WEEKEND MAKEOVER

Take Your Home from Messy to Magnificent
in Only 48 Hours!

OTHER DON ASLETT BOOKS
FROM ADAMS MEDIA

Clutter's Last Stand, 2nd Edition

Do I Dust or Vacuum First?, 2nd Edition

The Office Clutter Cure, 2nd Edition

Pet Clean-Up Made Easy, 2nd Edition

DONE! How to Accomplish Twice as Much in Half the Time—at Home and at the Office!

Help! Around the House: A Mother's Guide to Getting the Family to Pitch in and Clean Up

Is There Life After Housework? 2nd Edition

WEEKEND MAKEOVER

Take Your Home from Messy to Magnificent in Only 48 Hours!

DON ASLETT

America's #1 Cleaning Expert

Adams Media
Avon, Massachusetts

Published by Adams Media,
an F+W Publications Company
57 Littlefield Street
Avon, MA 02322
www.adamsmedia.com

ISBN: 1-59337-486-0
Printed in Canada.

J   I   H   G   F   E   D   C   B   A

Library of Congress Cataloging-in-Publication Data
Aslett, Don.
Weekend makeover : take your home from messy
to magnificent in only 48 hours! / Don Aslett.
p.   cm.
"Originally published under title: Lose 200 lbs. this weekend: its time to
declutter your life!."
ISBN 1-59337-486-0
1. House cleaning. I. Title.
TX324.A75837 2005
648'.5--dc22
2005026074

This publication is designed to provide accurate and authoritative information with
regard to the subject matter covered. It is sold with the understanding that the publisher
is not engaged in rendering legal, accounting, or other professional advice. If legal advice
or other expert assistance is required, the services of a competent professional person
should be sought.

—From a *Declaration of Principles* jointly adopted by a Committee of the
American Bar Association and a Committee of Publishers and Associations

Many of the designations used by manufacturers and sellers to distinguish their products
are claimed as trademarks. Where those designations appear in this book and Adams
Media was aware of a trademark claim, the designations have been printed with initial
capital letters.

Cover illustration by Tad Herr.
Interior illustrations by Jim Hunt.us

This book is available at quantity discounts for bulk purchases.
For information, please call 1-800-872-5627.

CONTENTS

Dear Readers:

Dear Don,
Whatever happened to that book you were going to write about how to lose 200 lbs. in a weekend?
We need more dejunking inspiration from Don Aslett!
Thank you for writing these great books.

Dear Don,
We need something to push us past 'almost.' We know we ought to dejunk, we want to do it, but we just can't quite get over the edge. We need a hard-line, excuse blocking, no-holds -barred convincer to push our clutter from 'gonna' to 'gone.'

What, another book on dejunking? Yes, and a much-needed one, too!

I'm the world's expert on this subject, the "too much" that burdens our lives—junk and clutter.

I started a cleaning business as a college freshman more than fifty years ago now. When I did my first book, the best-seller *Is There Life After Housework?* I showed readers how to save 75 percent of the time they spent cleaning. I also discovered that almost half of the time we think of as cleaning time is actually spent dealing with junk and clutter.

I got so many letters and calls about the third chapter of *Is There Life After Housework?*—which helped people identify and eliminate junk—that I went on to write *Clutter's Last Stand*, an entire book on the subject. It became a bestseller, too—the bible of the dejunking movement. To satisfy the surge of interest in junk and clutter that followed, I wrote another top-selling book on the subject, a more "hands on" decluttering guide called *For Packrats Only*. Then, because my company cleans hundreds of millions of square feet of office space a night, and I have worked in and around office buildings all my life, I wrote a book called *The Office Clutter Cure*, for the many people seriously oppressed by this type of clutter.

Letters, calls, and requests for information about junk and clutter continued to pour in, and I collected a wealth of real-life information on the subject—stories and testimonials, firsthand accounts of clutter cures and disasters, how-to and how-not-to anecdotes and accounts, pure gold from readers. I put the best of these into a book called *Clutter Free: Finally and Forever!*—a book of insight and guidance "straight from the horse's mouth," from the "confessions" of reformed clutterers.

I had four books on the subject, but every day and week new insights about clutter—and more and better information on coping with and coming to terms with it—arrived. I knew by now, too (because you kept telling me), that clutter sufferers need regular doses of "dejunking therapy." It was time for a new decluttering guide, one that would help packrats over perhaps the biggest stumbling block of all: "I really want to dejunk, but it's so hard to get started!"

So here is my latest dose of dejunking therapy. In addition to explaining how to dejunk in one weekend and showing you many good ways to go about getting it done, it has two important missions.

First, this book will convince and help you to dejunk *now, this upcoming weekend*. Most clutterers, even if they agree they should dejunk, have a real problem getting started and then following through. This book will provide the jump start you need to declutter *now*—not next year or "someday." It will show you how the all-important first big installment of the process can be fit into that little stretch of free time available to almost every one of us: one weekend. And you will learn how you can speed the process from there until every last bit of clutter is gone. This book also further develops a thread that appears in *Clutter's Last Stand,* to which my readers have responded with overwhelming enthusiasm: The mental and spiritual aspect of clutter—how decluttering your possessions and physical surroundings will relieve depression, stress, and anxiety, and make you feel peaceful and free.

In these pages you will find a simple solution for the two giants we are now battling: "too much" and "too busy." There is a clear link between too much clutter and too much to do, and improving the one will automatically improve the other. Lack of time, stress, and lack of space are three of our biggest complaints today, and decluttering will immediately relieve all of these.

Chapter 6 will even help you with the always-difficult "sifting and sorting" of things (are they junk or not?) by condensing what you need to know about each of the most common kinds of clutter onto a single page.

So now you have it—my newest and best book on the subject, guaranteed to make you hate "stuff" more than ever.

Happy decluttering,

Don Aslett

Introduction

What You Are About to Read . . .

. . . Is a revolutionary approach to losing the "weight" we are sick of—ALL OF IT! Not just the weight around us (closet, attic, and garage clutter), but the weight (stress, pressure, and anxiety) that junk burdens our minds with. Being an expert on that first one—the weight around us, our junk and clutter—I know that if you knock it out of your life this weekend, it will do a lot to eliminate the other. It will work, I promise you.

So to get you started on the path to the freedom you've been seeking so long, this book is a short course in removing clutter from all areas of your home and grounds.

Why Dejunk?

If you need a reason, let me give you the big one: I was asked once on a major television talk show, "Why dejunk?" The first and only thing that popped into my head at that moment was "to eliminate mess and disorganization from your life." Later, I started a list of reasons to dejunk:

- For space
- To save time and money
- To create a more pleasant environment for ourselves
- To cut waste and help care for our planet better
- To improve appearance, health, and safety
- To be treated better
- For the "carryover" into all the other areas of our lives

My list of reasons, all very good ones, is still growing. But one reason to declutter your life has emerged as the *big number one:* You dejunk your place and yourself *to feel better!*

You've heard all kinds of promises and strategies for shedding the "too much" we all suffer from, but I'm asking you to do only one thing, which will take care of many.

Think a minute—if you knew that doing only one single thing would:

1. Lift that weight off your mind and shoulders
2. Up your self-esteem
3. Make you much more efficient
4. Give you more space (physical and emotional) to move
5. Save you money
6. Bring you peace and relaxation
7. Help you become more spiritual
8. Gain the respect and confidence of others
9. Cut your cleaning time 40 percent or more
10. Give you back hours, days, and years worth of time

And it wouldn't cost you anything, would you do it? Of course you would, and that's what this book is about!

The Voices That Come Out from Under Clutter

I get letters and calls every day about the effect of "stuff" on our lives and stamina. Let me share a few excerpts here to put you in the mood:

> "I never considered myself to be a packrat, just someone very short of time for keeping things orderly. But I must admit my house is a disaster area and a source of shame, embarrassment, and even depression for me."

> "My mom needs help. A long time ago, we waited and waited to give our pedigreed dog a haircut. She was pretty matted by the time we did get around to it, so badly in fact, that the hair all stuck together, in one piece or pelt as it appeared. It could almost stand up by itself! We still have it, and man, is it ugly!"

> "I bought a 35-foot-long conference table. It was a beautiful thing, must have cost $5,000–$10,000 to build. I had to hire a trailer and truck, and four people, to deliver it to my place of business. I've had it in the warehouse now for five years . . . will sell for $100."

> "We are just married and recently we moved 6,000 pounds of stuff to our new home, and we have no furniture yet. It was three times what the mover had estimated. . . . "

A man brought a traffic light home, and his wife yelled, "That's enough, get it out of here!" He took it out and traded it for a wagon wheel.

"Aunt Mildred has accumulated about 500 pounds of fabric over the years. She's moved it several times, and now has it stored on a sun porch across from her sewing room. Most of it is in colors too ugly to use."

"When we went through my aunt's stuff, there was a box of empty Scotch tape dispensers (the thin plastic throwaway type). That was bad enough, but when we dug deeper, we found another box full of broken spent Scotch tape dispensers."

"My grandmother saved all the little foam trays meat comes in at the supermarket."

Found in one suburban living room: old deer hide, a cream separator, and sheep shears.

"I can't believe it. I save the Chiquita banana stickers!"

"Gads, I have a collection of snowballs in my freezer and 300 hats in my closet."

"I have 50 years of *National Geographics*. Trouble is, the mice and rats have eaten all of the glue on the bindings, so now there are no separate issues, just one giant *National Geographic*."

One woman accumulated more than 2,000 empty plastic milk jugs and stored them strung on twine hung from the barn rafters. You never know, you might need them to fill with sand and use for tent pegs.

"Oops, gotta go. My crowded recipe files are calling my name, and the wine bottles I save to make herbal vinegar are fighting in the cupboard corners behind my turntable (and I'm out there piling in more)."

"You've talked about the most cluttered professions and I think 'teacher' is definitely one. An associate of mine, an art teacher, has almost worn out a shredder trying to get rid of old student papers and lesson plans she kept. My aunt and uncle are both retired from teaching, so I know. 'CPA' would have to be next."

"A hospital hired me to run a medical office in a rural community. Their warning that there would be some cleanup work involved was an understatement. There were shelves of medical journals in the basement that dated back more than twenty years. The physicians told me, 'We never use them. We just keep them in case we might need them.' Upstairs in the physicians' office I found antique instruments in drawers that had not been touched for decades. I found expired drugs that no one had ever bothered to throw away. There were three huge cabinets with all sorts of medical supplies jammed in so tight that when you opened the doors everything fell out. One receptionist had four desktop calendars, and even the newest one was ten years old. Pile after pile of junk mail that 'might come in handy someday.' The hardest part about the cleanup was believing that this was an actual working doctors' office!"

"Packrat-ism is definitely genetic in nature. When my mother moved from her home, I found flower seeds that my father had saved from the year of my high school graduation twenty-five years ago. He stored seeds so well that he'd forget he had them, so he ended up buying new. I have inherited the gene from my father, but my need is to own multiples of everything: wooden spoons, knitting needle sets, boxes of Christmas cards, backpacks, even cats."

What Kind of Junker Are You?

You might be surprised to know there are more than 300 kinds of hummingbirds, and more than 300,000 kinds of beetles. But junkers are a flourishing family, too. They come in many species and subspecies, variants, and types. Which kind of junker are you?

Find yourself—check the following categories that seem familiar or fitting. This is just for fun, but be honest!

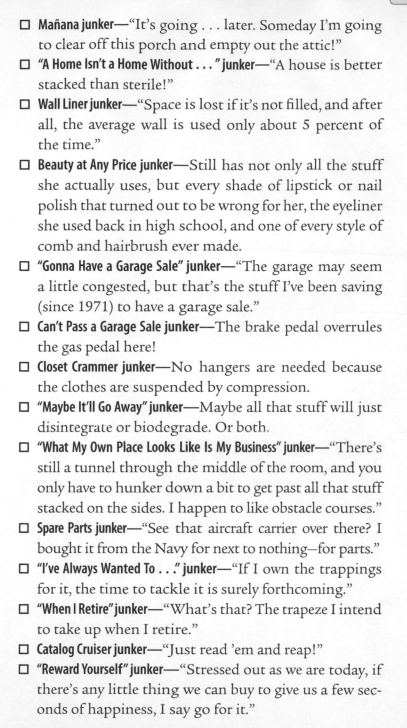

- ☐ **Mañana junker**—"It's going . . . later. Someday I'm going to clear off this porch and empty out the attic!"

- ☐ **"A Home Isn't a Home Without . . . " junker**—"A house is better stacked than sterile!"

- ☐ **Wall Liner junker**—"Space is lost if it's not filled, and after all, the average wall is used only about 5 percent of the time."

- ☐ **Beauty at Any Price junker**—Still has not only all the stuff she actually uses, but every shade of lipstick or nail polish that turned out to be wrong for her, the eyeliner she used back in high school, and one of every style of comb and hairbrush ever made.

- ☐ **"Gonna Have a Garage Sale" junker**—"The garage may seem a little congested, but that's the stuff I've been saving (since 1971) to have a garage sale."

- ☐ **Can't Pass a Garage Sale junker**—The brake pedal overrules the gas pedal here!

- ☐ **Closet Crammer junker**—No hangers are needed because the clothes are suspended by compression.

- ☐ **"Maybe It'll Go Away" junker**—Maybe all that stuff will just disintegrate or biodegrade. Or both.

- ☐ **"What My Own Place Looks Like Is My Business" junker**—"There's still a tunnel through the middle of the room, and you only have to hunker down a bit to get past all that stuff stacked on the sides. I happen to like obstacle courses."

- ☐ **Spare Parts junker**—"See that aircraft carrier over there? I bought it from the Navy for next to nothing—for parts."

- ☐ **"I've Always Wanted To . . ." junker**—"If I own the trappings for it, the time to tackle it is surely forthcoming."

- ☐ **"When I Retire" junker**—"What's that? The trapeze I intend to take up when I retire."

- ☐ **Catalog Cruiser junker**—"Just read 'em and reap!"

- ☐ **"Reward Yourself" junker**—"Stressed out as we are today, if there's any little thing we can buy to give us a few seconds of happiness, I say go for it."

- ☐ **Home in My Purse junker**—"The doctor says this droop in my right shoulder can be easily corrected, by attaching a fifteen-pound weight to the other side for a while, to even things out."
- ☐ **"Gotta Be Prepared" junker**—"This harpoon is hard to fit into some of my suitcases, but if I ever find myself stranded in the middle of the ocean I'll be glad to have it."
- ☐ **"I Was There" junker**—"Behold—a genuine Keep Off the Grass sign from Glacier National Park, a petrified praline candy from New Orleans, and barnacles from Plymouth Rock!"
- ☐ **"I Can Afford It" junker**—" . . . Between that lower credit card interest and all the money I'm going to save when I stop smoking."
- ☐ **"What Junk?" junker**—"It's an important resource!"
- ☐ **"Married to a Packrat" junker**—"My stuff, of course, is all good stuff."
- ☐ **"Don't Know Where It All Came From" junker**—"I was wondering about that myself, on the way home from the flea market."
- ☐ **Early Start junker**—"Got my early training saving bubble gum wrappers and bottle caps, until I was old enough to move on to Barbie accessories."
- ☐ **"I'm a Collector" junker**—"The minute I get a second one of anything, it starts a new collection."
- ☐ **Eclectic junker**—"I'm very selective . . . I'll just take this, this, and this . . . "
- ☐ **Live to Shop junker**—There's only one stopper—death!
- ☐ **Ridiculous junker**—You have it, but you can't explain it.
- ☐ **Inheritance junker**—"Where there's a will there's a way, to save everything that was left for you!"
- ☐ **After the Divorce junker**—Evidence! Sentiment! Revenge!
- ☐ **Real Estate junker**—"I don't want all the land in the world, just all that borders me."

☐ **Craft Accumulator junker**—"Cute, cuddly, one of a kind—it's a keeper!"

☐ **Great Buy junker**—"If the price is right, it's right!"

☐ **"It Was 'Free'" junker**—There's a lot of free cheese in a mousetrap, too.

☐ **"My Parents Were Much Worse" junker**—"If you think I'm bad, you should have seen their ball of string."

☐ **"I've Got the Room" junker**—"If you've got it, fill it! What's a few more dozen empty quart jars (even if I never can)?"

☐ **"You Name It, I Have It" junker**—He could outfit any expedition, win any scavenger hunt. And he's proud of it.

☐ **Enough Is Never Enough junker**—"Maybe Rubbermaid will start making 100-gallon containers."

☐ **"They Don't Make Them Like This Anymore" junker**—"Do you realize this thing (whatever it is) is made of solid cast iron?"

☐ **"It May Be Worth a Lot Someday" junker**—"It's bound to become a collector's item . . . someday!"

☐ **"I'll Decide Later" junker**—"I'm not sure whether I really need this leaky old air mattress or not, so I'll just set it down with all those other To Be Decided Laters there (as soon as I find a scaffold to reach the top of the pile)."

☐ **Depression Days junker**—Saves everything, because you just never know when there might be another Depression. (If it was a BIG enough depression, he could bury all that old worn-out stuff in it and live happily ever after.)

☐ **"I Might Need It Someday" junker**—"There might not be much call for a corset tightener on a day-to-day basis, but you never know . . . "

☐ **"I'll Think of a Use for It" junker**—"Don't throw it away! I'll figure out a use for it sometime (and besides, that little doohickey on top is really cute, isn't it?)."

☐ **"Can't Admit I Made a Mistake" junker**—"They do take up a lot of my storage space. But I got them for only $60!"

☐ **"I'm Sentimental" junker**—"That's a maraschino cherry from the first sundae we ever shared, an aphid from my wedding bouquet, and a freeze-dried pea from the chicken a la king we served at the reception."

☐ **Evidence junker**—"The way I see it—baby's first step or first time you were ever stood up—if you don't have real hard evidence of it, it didn't happen."

☐ **Tradition junker**—"Everyone in my family has one of these, and I already have one saved for each of my great-grandchildren."

☐ **Clothes Keeper junker**—"I call this wing of the house my walk-around closet."

☐ **Paper Piler junker**—"It may look bad in here, but don't worry, I know where everything is."

☐ **Environmentally Aware junker**—"I certainly don't intend to do anything to exacerbate the national landfill overload."

☐ **Check the Curb junker**—"You wouldn't believe some of the things people throw away. Just last week I found a perfectly good bowling ball with only 2 holes plugged."

Clutter Health Score Chart

Count up the checks you made and rate yourself below.

0 checks: YOU ARE PURE! Give this book to an overloaded friend.

1-3 checks: You are only mildly infected, but watch it!

4-6 checks: The balance is tipping in the wrong direction!

7-12 checks: You are badly cluttered and contagious—stay home and dejunk!

13-20 checks: You are out of room, and may soon be out of patience.

21-30 checks: It's not too soon to panic.

31 checks and up: You may be a lost cause. Start a swap meet or open a junker store.

Chapter 1

Too Much!

There comes a day (maybe it's here—maybe it's coming soon—maybe it happened a long time ago?) when your intake takes over, when all that you've bought and brought home catches up with you. You are totally occupied taking things in and taking care of them. First you pay for it all; later, you organize it, and then you frantically try to control it. Finally, life seems to be down to just fighting it. It's all pure weight on, in, and all around you. It's yours, you own it, and you are constantly tending it. Cuss it or call it anything you like—it is excess, "too much," clutter.

Not only is all this now taking away your happiness and popularity, but it's taking up room. It's interesting how the consequence of consuming is the loss of not just money but your space, both physical and mental. Yet, how we struggled and paid to gain all this stuff.

A High Standard of Luxury, Not Living

Who told us that all of this stuff we've acquired would create a high standard of living? Worrying about it and fighting and finagling to pay for the "too much" we now have piled everywhere is not a high standard of living. It's a real case of mislabeling. The only thing we really have here is a high standard of luxury.

A high standard of living is:

- Freedom
- Good health
- Good friends
- High self-esteem
- Being debt-free
- A stable and happy family
- A satisfying marriage

A high standard of luxury is having all the conveniences and comforts we think will eliminate effort and strain—those gadgets and extras of all kinds they keep coming up with and we keep accumulating.

In the 1980s, for instance, Dick Tracy's old two-way radio wristwatch gave way to handheld or pocket-size electronic devices of all kinds. There wasn't a worry or need in life not covered by a portable phone, beeper, pager, radio, camera, exercise device, memory jogger, organizer, laptop computer, calculator, or thesaurus. By the 1990s we had mobile message recorders; note recorders; electronic translators; portable shredders; CD players; blood pressure monitors; personal protection devices; garage door openers; white noise generators; navigation guidance systems; electronic binoculars, and key finders. Soon there were portable media centers, cell phones with built-in cameras, handheld DVD players, and more.

We call ourselves consumers but we don't actually consume. We just keep on purchasing and piling.

Convenience is often a clutter now, too much to manage—we can't even manage the stuff sold to help us manage. We are always fighting complications, and it is really the "too much" that complicates.

Luxury doesn't come without a big price tag and lots of stuff that "sticks" to us. We are now spending much of our time and money trying to recover from or remove the "too much" in, on, and around us. Millions and millions of us are buying every new storage expander or organizing device that comes along, books, tapes, seminars, programs, plans, rental storage units, trips to faraway places, pills, and sessions at the shrink. We're doing all this not to live life to its fullest, but to get relief, to be released from or rid of the "too much."

Truly it is pathetic and scary!

We Have Everything!

A successful Southern California bank retained me to speak to all its employees once and took me to dinner at a fancy restaurant with a number of those employees first. After dessert, a conversation about economic conditions ensued. The bank president, exploring my opinions, finally asked me one of those questions we all ask and all have definite ideas on: "Don, what do you think is wrong with the economy?"

The table went quiet as all the financial geniuses turned to me, Idaho's Businessman of the Year, for a profound answer. I cleared my throat and made some strong remarks about education, labor, government, and attitude in the workforce. My reasoning was pretty good I thought, but apparently it didn't impress the president.

"No, that isn't it," he said. "What's wrong with the economy is, we have everything. *We have everything!*" he said, and then proceeded to go around the table, asking tellers, bank officers, passing waitresses and busboys, etc., questions like, "How many microwaves, televisions, radios, pairs of shoes, CD players, recliners, watches, and automobiles do you own?" He grilled us all on every possible thing one could need or own, and we all had not only one, but most of us more than one. "Don, if people had all the money in the world, what else would they buy? We have everything."

For the next few months and the whole year following, his comment stayed in the back of my mind, and it seemed to apply to most of the situations and problems that cropped up. The negatives don't come from lack of things or commodities, they come from too much. We are overloaded with tangibles—the shortages we are feeling are in time, love, attention, and affection, all shorted because we don't have the time or money left over after all we have to tend.

A little while after this conversation, a Detroit publicity assistant who was driving me to a television show mentioned that she worked in the malls as a salesperson during the Christmas holidays. "You know, Don," she said, "almost every customer looking for gifts ends up buying something that someone already has. Friends and family have everything, so

they have to purchase a duplicate—an updated, different, or deluxe model."

Right she is! My wife and I have six children we thought we raised frugally—and none of them are what you would call well-heeled now. Last Christmas my wife and I struggled and searched to get them something they don't already have (we consider ourselves creative people), and generally they had two or three of whatever we came up with.

"What about a watch?" I suggested for one of the grand-children. That got chuckles. When I was young we would finally get a watch for high school graduation or, often, college. These days, kids at eighth-grade graduation don't need a watch—they have three or four already kicking around their room. Ten-dollar digital, TV-character watches that we couldn't even comprehend in the old days, the "less" days. Not to mention in those same kids' rooms you'll now find disks, players, and accessories for every type of video game system around, and the minute a new one comes out, all the old ones become obsolete and we have to buy them brand-new ones.

I constantly see kids pawing through a closet that would fill at least one aisle of the local mart, whining and whimpering that they have "nothing to wear," lounging around and griping, picking on parents who bought them that too much.

Go to your drawers and closets and you will see the same thing—TOO MUCH!

In the old days, we were held in control somewhat by the one-room cabins, one-room schoolhouses, and houses with few closets and no attached garage. But today, many of the new houses going up have three-car garages, and many of the buildings we see going up are "storage rentals," one of the most booming businesses.

We are now in a time of accelerated acquisition of stuff. It once took years and years to accumulate a houseful. Young married couples now can easily overspend and overown, and use those all-too-convenient credit cards to charge themselves into total submission to clutter before the age of forty, giving their lives over to craving, owning, and caring for too much.

It is almost unbelievable that now (without even a guilty conscience) we pay for a storage unit, a place to keep our run-over clutter away from home. If having a jammed, overflowing home is shameful, what would you call renting space and sheds elsewhere for junk?

Remember the "hope chests" women used to have, wherein they stored trinkets and treasures, napkins, and needlework for their future lives? Today those cedar containers wouldn't hold a week's worth of our "hope for the future" things. If those beautiful chests had been increased in size proportionate to our stuff, they would be bigger than a doublewide house trailer! There are not a few homes around in which there is so much stuff piled everywhere, in every room of the house, that there is only a path or trail from room to room.

Most of us have been led, swayed, and seduced into tending too much. We set our goals and work a lifetime to get it all, thinking it's a pleasure all the time that we're fighting it.

We hear a lot about youth, marriage, and employment problems, and when you look at what underlies the attitudes and arguments that cause so much trouble, it all boils down to those same two words: . . . TOO MUCH!

It is not uncommon for people to think their vehicle has been stolen out of a parking lot and then realize that they brought one of their other cars today, and forgot. . . . Again, a case of too much to keep track of. And many of us are waking up to realize we may be overhoused and overpropertied.

Once only the rich could own and buy more land and buildings than they needed; now many of us have "too much house." Banks have some pretty impressive qualifiers to determine if a buyer can or should buy a certain place—if the would-be purchaser can truly afford it. Their formulas and ratios of income to payment are well thought out and tested.

Yet when a bank or other lending institution comes back and tells someone he can't or doesn't qualify for financing on a place (it is too much for him to handle), what does he do? He goes to another bank and fibs and fudges, stretches and pads his financial statement, quietly borrows some down-payment money from his folks or others—anything to get him in that house. Thus hundreds of thousands of people end up with something that later comes back to haunt them (or they lose it) because they cannot sustain it—it is literally too much for them to tend.

With a strain or loss like this come additional strains to health and relationships . . . all for "too much."

Isn't our behavior shouting (gasping!) "too much"? Look at the:

1. Increase in closet, house, garage, and storage building size.
2. Increase in trash production (we're up to six pounds a day each, now).
3. Increase in installment payments of all kinds.
4. Increase in stress claims and complaints.
5. Increase in trips and vacations to relieve "burnout."
6. Growing numbers of people retreating to special-rate motels on the weekend, to get away from the home scene—bad!
7. Increase in the number of books, programs, and seminars for people who are dealing with the aftermath of overload—just check out the "Recovery" section of a bookstore.

There must be sixty different species of exercise bikes now—media advertisements, stores, and catalogs are filled with them. The racks and aisles of bookstores are crammed with tens of thousands of diet books. Yet recent studies have shown that we "health conscious" Americans are heavier than ever—more than 60 percent of us are overweight! And as for that "stuff" we own, store, and compulsively collect, just take a drive past those homes with three-car garages and see all three cars parked outside in the winter. Or take note of the acres and acres of storage units, or peruse all the new kinds of plastic containers and closet organizers. The big bottom line is simply . . . *too much*!

We who aren't entirely bloated yet can count on becoming so, because we are all on the line the banker summed up so well. We not only have everything, we are planning loans and credit line increases, trips, and scouting expeditions to get more, to finish burying ourselves.

A Day of Accelerated Acquisition and Accumulation

Two modern words that really expand our capacity for more and too much are convenience and access.

As we pass through a day, we are constantly reminded—in the mail, when we go online, by road signs, in newspapers and magazines, by television and radio commercials, and by phone solicitations—that all we have to do is touch a button, dial a number, or say "yes," and we can have ownership of almost anything. Everything is convenient, everything is accessible, and the principle of "afford" has been distorted to the point where it no longer means the ability to pay for something, it means the ability to acquire it immediately. With all of the credit plans and schemes and cards around today, whether we are rich or poor or in between, we can buy almost anything we want, whenever we want. We don't have to save and wait and consider it; we can, in an instant, *own it*! (And not feel the bite of the purchase immediately.)

It is a day of accelerated acquisition and accumulation. The average person has more material things and conveniences, more luxury, security, and comfort, than the wealthy did not long ago.

In this day of endless offers and almost-too-accessible objects, even the most positive things that we want, need, and use for pleasure, satisfaction, or our jobs have almost become a curse. Look at toys, sports and hobby equipment, furniture, and vehicles. They are so easy to buy and own now that all of us, for example, own multiple cameras, usually lying around unused. Just do an audit on your shoes, or your family's shoes! Our kids could leave a pair of shoes at each of four friend's homes and still have some to wear at home.

Has all this made us happy, satisfied? Well, at the time of acquisition, things do have some stimulant value, but when the honeymoon is over, the wrapping paper stops rattling, and the new things join our mounting pile of too much, they nag us, are expensive; we have no room to store them, and no time to tend them. Our too much begins to hurt instead of help, and we find ourselves shackled with stuff.

The Triangle of Too Much

We have so many things and comforts these days, yet
our level of personal satisfaction and happiness seems
to be lower than ever, which doesn't seem to make sense.
And the big three we are struggling with are:

1. Mental and emotional stress (clutter in us)
2. Overweight worries and concerns (clutter on us)
3. Our stuff: All the things and possessions of all kinds we have
   (the clutter around us)

These three form a monster triangle in our lives. We have too
much on our minds, too much on our midriffs, and too much in our
garages, basements, drawers, closets, and rental units. A flight
attendant, looking over my shoulder when I had a sketch of the
triangle of "too much" spread out in front of me, summed up the
problem: "Wow, it's the Bermuda Triangle of disfunctionality!"

A Sure Way to Reduce Stress

Isn't this a day of increasing stress and strains in families,
friendships, marriages, jobs, positions, and finances? It seems
everyone is searching for a way to reduce stress. Well think
how much stress—money, time, and emotion—is connected
with getting and looking after excess stuff.

A while ago, *Reader's Digest* quoted me in an article called
"Stress Proof Your Home." I received many calls and comments about it later, and most of the people who called said
that they had never before associated stress with "stuff."

We have "stuff stress"—so to relieve it, we go
out and get more stuff. Shedding excess stuff is
the surest, quickest way to shed stress.

I've made hundreds of "dejunking" appearances on radio and TV, run many decluttering seminars, answered thousands of letters and questions, and listened to as many phone calls and conversations about clutter as any breathing soul. I can give you the bottom line of my experiences and observations here in just three words of my own: EXCESS WILL DEPRESS. (Read more about the relationship between clutter and stress in Chapter 2!)

Too Much Means Too Busy

We are all battling two big things today: too much and too busy. Our lives have gone past "active" to a full-out sprint, and just getting through the day now is almost a battle of will. How often at the end of another day at home, work, or even play do we wonder what we did, why we did it, and where it is taking us? Often we're so rushed we don't remember where we've been or really notice where we are, and we begin to question where we are going. Ninety-five percent of people who evaluate their schedule and their storage areas are waking up to the fact that they are too busy and have too much to tend.

The majority of us are too busy *as a result* of too much. Cut the too much and you'll cut the too busy. Pretty simple! We can feel good about "much" or "busy" if it is blessing our life. If, on the other hand, it is stressing and straining you to the max, then **this weekend** is the right time to bail out.

*"Too much" causes much of the "too busy" in life,
so in reality we have only one giant in the battle
of life to fight and defeat—too much.*

That excess is not going to go away by itself, but this little manual will take care of one or more big loads of it. And once you get going, you won't want to stop. Most of the miracle weight-loss books, seminars, programs, and gimmicks are just increasing our load level, taking our money and space without taking an ounce off us. In these pages you will find a quick diet that really works. Most of us need to, most of us want to, and all of us *can* lose that excess around us.

Just One Weekend Will Get You Started

All you need is just one weekend to start . . . and you'll gladly give several more toward a glorious finish. Just find yourself one clear weekend. Stand in front of and behold all of your STUFF . . . and begin. Chapters 4 and 5 will tell you what you need to know about how to go about it. I will tell you how to come to terms with too much—explain the whats, whys, and whens of decluttering, to gain back some space and lots more.

Was there ever a time in your life when the weeds and grass of your lawn got longer and longer, . . . weekend after weekend went by and you knew you should get at it, but you didn't? Then, when you finally did get started and saw all that ugly old grass go down and the trim, fresh, clean result, you just couldn't be stopped from doing as much as you could that weekend? I promise that you'll easily lose a hundred pounds or more of your stuff this first weekend. (You may even lose an inch or so off your waist if you don't eat those moldy old chocolates that have been stashed under the videos since Halloween.) This first weekend will be the jump-start to get your motor running, and once it starts running, it will generate the power and voltage to carry on. If you really give this a good first weekend, any other weekends you need to finish the job will come naturally. . . . And best of all, you won't be out buying anything more! Go for it!

An Extra Bonus of the Weekend Plan

Thoughts and habits and behavior—be it a bad temper or a big appetite—are not easy to change. Most of us know what is wrong already; we are all too aware of our too much's and don't wants. So having some saintly solution-giver come along and tell us:

- Eat less!
- Don't get mad
- Don't gossip or lie
- Don't lust or covet

. . . seldom makes us change. Few can walk out of a seminar or counselor's office and just quit some unpopular habit or behavior. No matter how much they are bothering us, or how badly we want to stop them, habits hang on, don't they? Look at how long and from how many angles we have been working on some of these things, and still are.

I'm convinced that the majority of the clutter in our minds (and even any excess weight we have on our person) evolves from what is around us. Our stuff sires the sorry too much of calorie clutter and mental disarray, too. What we own, nurture, and tend, we absorb and become like. An overload of stuff overloads the circuits of the body and the brain. So let's use this fact to our advantage, to reverse the process. Instead of starting our fight with the emotional, let's start with the stuff. We are less attached to it and it is less attached to us. All that stuff around us is much easier to kick out than the stuff in and on us.

There is an amazing discovery you will make here. When you dump a physical or tangible possession, a thing, a piece, or a part of all that is piled in your place, you experience a tiny taste of freedom, space, and dominion. Remove more and you get more good feelings and a delightful sensation of weightlessness. Then a sweet, clean spirit of purity will sweep into your character and a sense of control will come to you, an assurance that "I don't need excess to be happy." And the clean area will start whispering a beautiful song of freedom to you that will inspire and motivate you to keep going.

The pleasures of being clutter-free will carry over into every area of your life!

> "You have given me motivation and direction for putting my office, home, and life in order. One great benefit has already started happening—I'm losing weight! I'm not sitting around eating because I feel overwhelmed, unmotivated, and without direction."

So just forget about the brain and body weight right now and go for the excess stuff around you. When it goes (and it can quite easily), it will reduce, quietly and naturally, any problems you may have with what you eat, drink, and think.

The Magic Word That Can Completely Change Your Life

Is there one pill, phrase, or simple process that will enable us to change our lives, to be where and what we really want to be? I believe it is "less." By the time you finish this book, I think you'll agree. The more of the unnecessary we release, the more of the beautiful we find. If things get ever more complicated and confusing, at home and at work, it is because the whole focus of society is more—the exact opposite of less.

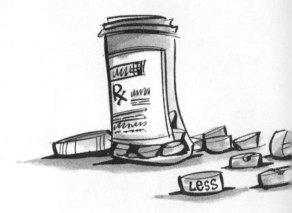

Chapter 2

Just What Are the Costs of Clutter?

We all admit that the excess around us is inflicting some damage, but just how much? We may not have noticed, because we've gotten used to the labor and frustration of trying to squeeze more into a "no more" space. Or maybe our payment is in such subtle installments that we haven't done an accurate balance sheet on it. Let's take a look at some of those payments now. What does that "too much" do to us?

It Makes Us Run in Circles

The biggest pain of possession is the vicious circles we end up milling in: Filling the garage until we are forced to dejunk it, cramming the closet until we finally have to excavate in there. Gadfrey, aren't we the experts at doing all we can to cause a problem, then doing all we can to fix it?

The strongest and most stable of us end up here—the circle of getting in and getting out. We build big houses, loaded with comforts and conveniences, and then spend all our time on the road and in the shops. We pay dearly to possess things and haul them home, and then pay to get rid of them. We junk and clutter ourselves into debt and then take desperate measures to get out.

The Vicious Circle of Clutter

Getting it, owning it, inventorying it, organizing it, attempting to control it, dumping it . . . getting it, etc. This circle of futility doesn't only wear us out—it weighs us down.

Most, if not all, of us are in this race, trying to get and own all we can as fast as we can. We're surrendering some of the finest time and opportunities of our lives right now for the pretty stuff, the glittery stuff (stylish, fashionable, elegant, bigger, better, more). We joke about and shake our heads over neighbors who are building bigger houses farther up the hill, going for just a little more square footage and altitude for a little more prestige, . . . while most of us are doing exactly the same thing!

We've all seen those headlines: "Families Running in Overtime." Where and for what? Mostly to sustain stuff. A couple of ordinary everyday people I know were summing up their present endeavors and life accomplishments and both agreed that just "making ends meet" occupied every waking hour. Both are a lot more knowledgeable now than when they were young, both have a nice family and a much greater income than when they were young, but they still aren't getting what they really want because paying for all of the extras they bought consumes them.

Trying to describe her now-hectic life, one woman said it well: "I always did have a list of things to do and tend to, but today the list is so much longer." She was doing more but not feeling any more rewarded with life, because most of the "to do today" stuff on her list amounted to caring for, accounting for, and accumulating more stuff.

"Carefree Consumption"—a lie

Amazing, isn't it, this circle of too much? It's not a good place to be if you want a happy, freer life anytime soon.

Clutter Makes Us Feel Hopeless and Depressed

Many a packrat has said, "Sometimes . . . I feel I am a lost cause." No one is a lost cause. I believe this lost sensation is largely caused by trying to squeeze good things out of artificial things, or by looking for love in all the "lots" places. So we buy more, travel more, own more, accumulate more—gadgets, machines, collectibles, knickknacks, furnishings—yet we cannot seem to find what we're looking for anywhere. This is where the lost feelings originate: with too much stuff. The struggle to maintain our ethics and productivity meets enough obstacles in life, and when you're weighed down by stuff you don't really need, want, or like (but you possess), you will get a real feeling of hopelessness.

Katharine Hepburn had a great line in *Love Affair:* "The trick in life isn't getting what you want. . . it's wanting it after you get it."

There are thousands of destressing seminars and therapy sessions going on right now, as you read this—stress management; stress analysis; stress control; stress in the family, marriage, and business; teen stress; and team stress. In all of the solutions—ranging from coping to cutting out—I've yet to see one that hits the biggest stressor head-on.

I think destressing boils down to one word: dejunk! We do have to handle the necessary, but most of us are lugging along hundreds or even thousands of pounds of the unnecessary—all of which is competing for time and space with the necessary. Most of us aren't disorganized like we think, we are just overloaded with the unnecessary, and we know it, too, and that is what is stressing us.

No matter how ingeniously it's done, all that time and energy expended on overload management is not really a progressive process. Before you know it, you are back again to fighting and coping with the strain and disorder of too much stuff, supporting it and paying for it and tending it, insuring it and heating it and dividing it and moving it and storing it and visiting it and arguing over it—all this unneeded and unused stuff.

Destress = Dejunk!

The Vocabulary of Excess

Just glance through all these words that relate to having too much. Isn't there an undercurrent of ugliness and harassment in most of them?

- Piles
- Stacks
- Hoards

- Heaps
- Rat's nest
- Cram
- Crush
- Overcrowded
- Overstuffed
- Bulging
- Overflowing
- Encumbered
- Loaded
- Laden
- Burdened
- Haul
- Excess baggage
- Rummage
- Muddle
- Confusion
- Unsettle
- Distract
- Disrupt
- Complicate
- Disorganized

- Chaos
- Jumble
- Mishmash
- Upset
- Perplexed
- Anxious
- Overwhelmed
- Bewildered
- Flustered
- Frustrated
- Embarrassed
- Disturbed
- Worried

- Mix-up
- Mess-up
- Entangle
- Millstone
- Disarray
- Saddle
- Balance due
- Overdraft
- Tax

Too much just mashes and mangles you constantly.

Clutter Makes Us Fight All the Time

I've noticed that among the thousands of people I've known or worked with in business, family, or the community, the most unhappy and unsuccessful people always seem to be battling something. Just listen to their conversations—every day is a fight with their spouses, their neighbors, their weight, their competitors, the cleaning, and so on. And more and more I hear people battling with their stuff. Folks are fighting to find a place for things, fighting the stuff in their way everywhere, fighting to pay for things they didn't really need. When your hands and feet and brain and energy and space are being used to fight, you have little left over to gain ground. If you've ever wondered what and why you are fighting all the time, it is generally excess—or something caused by excess.

Believe history! Too much has been the cause of most of
the problems of mankind, period! Medical history, military
history, sports history, entertainment history, religious
history—read it and weep, read it and don't keep!

Clutter Takes Away Our Freedom

What is it that men and women have hunted, schemed, sacrificed, and, yes, died for, for thousands of years now? Freedom. We figure out fast that freedom is "it"—a free country, and freedom in personal choices of all kinds, including ownership. Almost all wars, and, for that matter, person-to-person conflicts, have been over someone losing or taking away freedom.

Yet how readily we sacrifice our freedom to what that very freedom enables us to get. When people finally get to the point where they are free to make their own choices and no one can shove them around, they let *stuff* shove them around, and even out of their home and yard. And yes, even out of relationships.

The Invisible Handcuffs of Clutter

There is a slow and insidious transition here, from when you have things to when they have you. It's terrible to wake up one day and realize that something we think we own, in fact owns us! As one of my readers noted, "Junk kept me in one place; I couldn't move because I had too much to move."

A man I know wore a brightly colored T-shirt with an American flag on it, and in big letters it proclaimed, HOME OF THE FREE. About the only freedom the fellow had was the right to wear the shirt. He was immobilized by debt (owning too much), and as he put it, "I have no time." He had no space in or around his house, either. He had so much in the way of the chance to do any *living* that he had no freedom—and the jailer who had captured and was holding him was himself.

We see this everywhere today—people walking down the aisle of life filling their carts with gadgets and goodies, the carrying and keeping of which will cost them their freedom. Ironic, isn't it, that the enemy here isn't something wicked or ugly, but "nice things"—shiny, pretty, sensual. Don't we all work toward and fall for the "nicer" stuff, and then when we finally possess it—the best, the nicest—the less we share it, the more protective we get, the higher the insurance fees and the fences and the pitch of our voices looking for it when it is misplaced? And yes, *the less we use it.* The nicer the home and the more perfectly it is proportioned, the less time we spend in it.

It All Boils Down to, Are You Living to Have or to Become?

We've been sold the idea that living is having, when in fact, living is being, and the biggest "being" of all is being free from the weight of possessions, of things that push us down instead of elevate us.

The best things in life are not things!

Clutter Wastes Our Time

"Time" is the prize we are all seeking right now in our lives. We have a hundred times as many things and activities competing for our time than was the case in the old days. It isn't a question of serving two masters anymore, it is serving 200, and we can't do it all and still have anything akin to a quality life. The best way to zero in on quality is to shed the unnecessary. People trying desperately to "get it together" often start at the wrong end by searching out and adding ever more to their lives, when a much easier and more logical approach is simply eliminating what you don't need.

"We have six children and we home school, so there's plenty for me to do. But after rereading your books, I came to realize that

> schooling my children, sharing things with my husband, caring for our home, living my life—everything—was actually a sideline; my main occupation was moving clutter around, getting rid of it, trying to manage it somehow. I had devoted my entire life to this project!"

"Too Much" Doesn't Tend Itself

You don't just "have" anything, even if you are rich and can easily pay for it, or if it was a gift, or if you own Acme Storage, Inc. Stuff doesn't just sit there innocently in a drawer, closet, or storage unit. Stuff brings responsibilities—just like having a big family, a lot of land, a big business, or many community or religious commitments. More of a truism hasn't been spoken than when someone says, "Boy, this cost me an arm and a leg!" It actually did, because stuff takes arms to care for and carry it all, and legs to run and fetch and stumble over it. The cost of tending isn't just in the physical maintenance, either; it's a personal cost too. Tending kids—babysitting—is worthwhile because kids are our life and our heritage, an extension of ourselves. But tending stuff is just "maybe-sitting." We hire someone to sit our kids while we are out, but whether we're at home or out, we are sitting our clutter—our family of "too much"—all the time!

How Much Time Do You Lose to Clutter?

At least 40 percent of all our home cleaning, care, and maintenance time is spent on junk and clutter—cleaning it, and cleaning around, under, and through it. Not to mention all the time we spend buying it, storing it, moving it around, and pawing through it. It's hard to find love, joy, and edification with your head in a cubbyhole and your hands hunting and rummaging for "something."

Wouldn't it be interesting to have an accurate total of how many years of our life we spend fighting and tending and handling plain old junk and clutter? I've been on TV with expert "time scientists" who have taken polls and measurements to prove, for example, that we spend five years in lines, three years in meetings, four years eating, five years doing housework, four hours a day watching TV, and so on. I'll bet that if all of the time we devote to clutter were measured, extracting it as necessary from some of these other totals, it would be more than ten years of our lives.

Dejunking Will Mean You Never Have to Dig!

How much of your life are you spending searching for something buried or misplaced, or just somewhere in the giant pile? How many times a day do you say, "I'll see if I can find it"? Some people seem to spend most of their time thrashing through bags and purses and boxes and drawers in their homes and offices. If you dejunk only for the reason of never having to hunt, dig, or even look for something again, that would be enough of a reason to declutter yourself right now. The frustration of "misplaced" can be all but eliminated when there is less clutter around for things to blend into, slip behind, or get buried under. Good stuff buried under bad stuff becomes worthless also—you might as well not own anything.

Ever stop to count up the times people say, "I put it away and forgot I had it"? As one reader noted, "A couple of years ago we were going on vacation, and before we went I hid most of my jewelry to protect it from thieves. I hid it so well in all of my piles that I still haven't found it. And I was worried about thieves!"

Dejunking Will Instantly Improve Your Time Management

When you teach or speak on time management these days, most of the audience has already been through several seminars or bestselling books on the subject, complete with secret techniques and shortcuts and catchy acronyms, and few end up managing time any better. As America's #1 expert on the subject, I can tell you that dejunking will do more to improve your "time management" than any other single thing will. When you cut the stuff, you cut the time used seeking it out, stockpiling it, insuring it, explaining it, and so on. Little did all those great management geniuses know what truth they were teaching when they advised their students, staff, or clients to run "lean and mean."

Clutter Makes Us Inefficient

Most of us will acknowledge that, indeed, you "can't take it with you" when you die, but we're often unaware that we're taking it with us mentally and physically everywhere now, and paying for that poundage. Clutter runs us on an obstacle course and renders us ineffective twenty-four hours of every day we own it—the more stuff the stiffer the course. Every day, we have to wrestle with all that; hunt and rummage through it; stumble over it; clean around it; tend, protect, and insure it; wait on it; and, worst of all, try to explain it to all those folks giving us the eye.

If we would only stop long enough to see how our clutter and the areas where we fail to function well are related, we would be motivated to cut the clutter.

If there is a bottom-line word for personal efficiency, it is "unobstructed." We can get a lot more done by getting things that really don't count much out of the way. What an easy way to improve—rather than having to learn or add a skill, we just do a little removing of that which we are forever having to wait on or skirt around. Clutter makes us zig and zag, and dig and sag.

Don't let anyone tell you that cluttered means creative. Anyone who is cluttered and creative will be twice as creative when she is uncluttered. There is seldom control or creativity in the midst of clutter—we are too preoccupied with digging. Dejunking isn't just getting rid of some unnecessary objects—it is getting control of your life.

Clutter Makes Everything Cumbersome

Ever think how the too much in our lives interferes with life itself? I thought of this while checking into a hotel once. This little slip of paper was on the bed:

```
Room 210

1. All entrances but the lobby are locked
   24 hours a day. Your room key will
   allow you access to all entrances.
2. Safeguard your key, and be sure to
   leave it with the cashier upon depar-
   ture. Do not leave it in your room
   or in the door. Do not give your key
   to others.
3. For additional security, utilize the
   deadbolt provided on the room door.
   This will prevent the door from
   being opened by a regular room key.
   As an additional precaution, please
   secure the safety chain lock.
4. Please remove valuables from your
   car and put them either in the trunk
   or in your guest room.
```

As I watched people scurrying through all the details and rituals of this to protect their valuables, I thought how none of these *things* are really valuable. The true valuables here are *you, your health* and *mind,* and *your free time,* all of which are consumed protecting your nonvaluables. What a pleasure it is to travel with no valuables. My $12.95 company logo watch tells perfect time and it can be left on the dresser or in a restroom. It keeps me on time, advertises a little, and if someone rips it off, it is a gain for publicity! I seldom lock my car—a thief would get tired looking in there for something worth stealing.

Clutter makes it almost impossible to just get up and go. The other day I could only shake my head as I watched our family, friends, and some employees load coolers of juice, pop, and snacks and gather up CDs, etc., for a trip that would probably be a total of three hours in air-conditioned cars and would pass thirty feet from several rest stops on the way. It took hours to assemble and organize this stuff. I remember the days when we filled a canvas water bag, hung it on the front fender, and in thirty seconds were on our way to fish or play. Now we use the fishing and play time to prepare, process, protect, and parade our stuff.

You cannot travel light with clutter.

My whole message here can be well illustrated by a common pastime called camping. Camping in its original form (with the Scouts or the family) was simple, affordable, and refreshing—something we all could do—and it didn't take much more than a couple of matches to spark the whole event. I recently received in the mail, unsolicited, a "camping" catalog detailing all the gear necessary to do camping right. There were 239 pages crammed with small print and pictures of sleeping bags, tents, packs, all kinds of different models of trail chairs, mess kits, pallets, coolers, stoves and stove accessories, showers, washbasins, saws, knives, sandals, hammocks, cushions, and pads, plus thirty-eight different styles of camping shoes and trail shorts to be in style. Unbelievable, how camping could spawn such a proliferation of gear. I counted the items and there were 1,600 different camping "necessities" in this one catalog. (Not counting the $32,000 SUV one gets for the purpose, with no money left over for insurance and gas!)

My wife summed it up well: "We have ten times the trappings now and only go camping about one-third as much." Another sad case wherein the weight and cost choke out the original purpose.

Clutter Takes Our SPACE!

Most of the people I'm meeting and teaching these days who are unhappy with their situation use the word "space" a lot—"I need some space," "I need my space to do my thing," etc. This is another very good reason to declutter. Most of us have finally run out of space, in our credenzas and our clothes closets, our homes and yards. Too much moved in so slowly, so glamorously, so respectably that we hardly realized our lives were full, let alone too tight. Our brains, bookshelves, and storage bins are overloaded, and we are all looking around for a place to put the new and meaningful when it finally pops in front of us.

The question of the century: Why do we live crowded?
(By clutter, schedules, habits, people.)

I went to visit a young couple not long ago. They have a huge house with three bedrooms, a full basement, and a three-car garage. They are only in their midthirties but their place was full everywhere. It was time to get a swing set for the toddlers, and there was actually no room on their big lot for it—because of the grill, the trampoline, the hot tub, the sun deck, the motor home, the boat, the three lawn mowers, the sports and exercise equipment, all their lawn furniture, and so on.

They couldn't make full use of their own home. They needed space for an important thing and simply didn't have it (and they had a ton of stuff in rented storage, too).

This isn't a unique case. Most of you reading this are in about the same situation. You have no space in your place, or in your emotions. All those things you own and have stacked around you—junk and clutter and decorations and doodads and treasures—all of this isn't crowding only your rooms and your surroundings, your body; it is crowding your personality and your mind, too. You feel cramped, crowded, almost crushed. "Too tight" is the close companion of "too much."

"Out of sight, out of mind?" Wrong. If you have it, it crowds you. Dejunk! Feel the splendor of spaciousness instead of the lag of "loaded"—this weekend!

Stuff Leads to Stuffing

Being a multimillion-mile traveler, I get to see "stuff" as not just a noun but as a verb. Nowadays on a plane, for instance, one is allowed two checked pieces of luggage and two carry-on bags. That is four bags per person, often for just a short trip. People once moved entire households across country in one wagon!

This overload of stuff... how bad is it? Bad enough to make us run out of house space, closet space, drawer space, yard space, rental space, okay... but right now, look how many of us are out of wall space, even to hang things.

Then there is the loading time, and I don't mean for what goes into the baggage compartment. The airlines have added people and trucks and they do that fast. But the loading inside the plane has gotten to be a real spectacle. People come down the aisle puffing and straining—those carry-on bags are so big now they're more like drag-alongs. The little storage compartments above the passenger seats in a plane are maybe twelve inches high, and on every flight, there are rows of wheezing, grunting, well-dressed people trying to stuff a bulky twenty-four-inch bag into that twelve-inch space and they don't quite manage it. Even after looking the situation over, they try it again. But it's like trying to pour a quart of milk into a cup.

When the flight attendant (shaking his head in disbelief) offers to take their bags and check them, someone always asks if *he* might be able to stuff a fifty-pound carry-on into that twenty-pound space. And then, it never fails, the passenger stands there looking wounded and disgusted because her bag has to be checked after all.

This is by far the best entertainment in travel, much better than the movies they play on long plane trips. It is also exactly why so many of us are red-faced and breathless in life, as we try to stuff thirty hours worth of tending too much into twenty-four hours of living. Traveling light has rewards that only a few of us are aware of right now.

Where Do I Put This?

When I was in New Orleans to speak at a convention, I noticed a fantastic art shop in the lobby of the hotel. The pieces in there were so good, I just stood at the window in disbelief. In the center of it all was a three-foot-high bronze statue of a cowboy and horse, in an action pose that took me back to my early life experiences on the ranch. It was marked down from $2,595 to $595—a steal for an original like that. I had cash in my pocket, so I could afford it, but bad as I wanted it, it was another case of "too much." I had nowhere to put it. My walls, floors, shelves, tabletops, and every-thing—just like yours—were full to the brim. I was out of room, so I wistfully walked away.

If we could turn the need for this book into one big question, it would be, "Where do I put this?" Be it a once-in-a-lifetime treasure or just another one of those "neat things," where is it going to go?

Clutter Costs Us Money

Aren't you about tired of spending your hard-earned money on stuff? Most of us are trying to get ahead, but ahead of what? Interesting to consider that most of our get-ahead endeavors are actually putting us behind.

> Your junk is the most expensive guest you'll ever put up, and it takes from your life rather than adds to it, as you imagined and intended when you kept it.

We often think of our stuff as incidental add-ons that just came along—as if all this were free and we are just keeping it around because it costs nothing. But here in the twenty-first century, nothing is free to get or free to keep—everything has not just a purchase price but storage cost, maintenance and security costs, taxes, interest, insurance, etc. All the costs of those "harmless, inexpensive" little storage units, those extra garages, or an extra 1,000 square feet added to a building to accommodate overflow will often add up to $500 a month or more. That's $6,000 a year, and $60,000 in ten years, and in twenty, if this same money were invested and used productively, it could make a $250,000 difference in your assets right now. That's why this weekend is almost too late—the minute you cut clutter, you cut the costs, trust me. A more profitable life will immediately begin to emerge.

We all want to get our money's worth and end up with something worth paying for. Even people with money to burn still want a good deal. We hate to pay for something that isn't going to serve or satisfy us, yet oddly we are paying much of our time, space, and emotions to an actual enemy that we own. We pay for what slows us down, shows us up, and slowly suffocates us.

A friend of mine, the owner of a company that makes those little backyard barns, sort of like overgrown doghouses, once said, "You know, Don, I sell lots of these at home shows for $2,000 or more, and people use them to store $200 worth of junk forever."

Clutter charges a huge interest that compounds continually.

The bottom line of it all keeps coming up. Keeping costs! And need we say who pays?

Junk Embarrasses Us

An older, very proper and religious woman I know found a stash of *Playboy* magazines while cleaning out an apartment. They were distasteful to her, but as a true junker she recognized value: Since they were in mint condition, they were too good to throw out. So she sacked them up to take to the local secondhand store. As she was crossing the street in a crowd where most of the people knew her, the bag gave way under the weight and the stack fanned out across the street. Everyone looked at the magazines, then at her, then at the magazines . . . One way or another, junk will always put you on the spot!

> We worry about a little weight gain on the hips, but what about the gains in our storage crypts? They're ten times as noticeable.

Daily, if not hourly, our "too much" is paraded in plain view of others and we continually find ourselves explaining it, justifying it, and apologizing for it.

Our Clutter Shows on Us

It speaks for and about us, all the time. Your junk may be "your business," but it's show-and-tell when it comes to the public and the rest of your household. Our closets, basements, garages, and shelves, and even the insides of our refrigerators, reveal our habits, tastes, and intentions; how organized we are; how soon we get around to things; and possibly even our love lines and life line! There isn't enough storage space or ingenious enough "organizers" to conceal the appearance and effects of clutter. You can't cover excess with carports, sheds, or curtains—it's ugly and it shows. Excess is embarrassing no matter how you look at it.

We All Want to Be Treated Better

I think the desire we all have today to "live lighter," to feel better, is only surpassed by one more intense desire—and that is to be treated better. We are breaking our butts to get people to like us better and treat us better, and even the official experts in human behavior will agree the urge to be loved and needed is the big bottom line. Again, ironically, a big part of the too much we have is the result of our efforts to be wanted and liked. We buy bigger, better, and more of everything because we think it will make us more attractive. And it reverses on us so subtly we can't see it.

One very big reason—my favorite of all reasons—to declutter, even more important than getting back our space, is *to be treated better*.

Fair or unfair, right or wrong, we treat cluttered people unkindly. Even we, who are overburdened ourselves, treat our fellow overloaders badly. Clutter suggests confusion, disorder, a lack of discipline, poor planning, and a situation that is "out of control." Just what do others think of us when we are constantly hunting and digging to find "it" buried in a closet, a desk, a storage compartment? Or when we scurry around like big greedy rats, hoarding and boarding a bunch of junk?

Our clutter has invisible speakers mounted everywhere: in our front yards and on our porches, in our living rooms and kitchens and offices, the trunks of our cars, our lockers, closets, and drawers. And those speakers trumpet out loud and clear to everyone, "Here comes a disorganized dork—I'm behind, I'm not in control, and I *can't make a decision, so go ahead and dump more on me. Don't give me a raise or a promotion; I can't handle what I've got."*

People who are always surrounded by stuff are a turnoff. We distrust them, criticize them, and pass them over. Even if we love them, their load makes peace and orderliness hard to come by. No doubt about it, clutter-free people get treated better, and are better off physically, spiritually, and economically.

Indecisive You? . . . Maybe Not!

Another reason to curtail "too much" is to get your decisiveness back. There is a strong possibility that those of us who feel too indecisive are wrong. Indecisiveness is not the problem—the problem is that we simply have too many options to choose from. Most of the people I know who label themselves "indecisive" are quick to decide on a course when they have only two to twenty choices. When they have 200 choices, they become a vacillating mass of jelly. Isn't this true of all of us?

I've been a licensed paint contractor for more than forty years. Back when the stores and brochures had thirteen basic colors (plus a few shades of beige), picking colors was easy, fun, and the house looked good afterward. Then selections were improved and we had thirty-three colors. Picking colors took longer and required two people to come to a decision, but the house still looked good afterward. Then, marvelous new "colorizing" machines made it easy to provide an array of 332 colors. Picking colors now was a two-trip counseling process, with an exasperated painter and people nervous about the results, but the house still looked good afterward.

Then the modern day of "too much" arrived, with 1,322 (or *more*) colors, and it was pure indecisive agony for everyone selling, buying, mixing, painting, and deciding how the house looked afterward.

Have you ever considered clutter a severer of relationships, destroyer of friends and family, even jobs? If the ruining of marriages, family relationships, businesses, and clubs could be traced to its origin, we would often find that it was a focus on excess.

Clothes, cars, computers, tools, furniture, menu items—almost everything today—has multiplied in models and options similarly, and this has complicated the selection and collection process. But you *can* decide, once you can see over the top of the heap. When you have only the things in your closet and toolbox that you really want and use, and when you look on only the page of the catalog that has what you actually need, you won't be caught up in endless debating and deciding.

An Altruistic Reason to Dejunk

Now, in the reasons to get rid of the clutter in our lives, comes the issue of "other people." For a change, let's stop thinking of how our clutter, our depression, or our disarray harms and irritates us, and instead consider the other people with and around us. What effect does our excess have on those we know and love—how does it affect the quality of their lives?

For starters, our condition gives a clear message of how much we cherish "things," and it is often at the expense of others in our lives, of the time we have to be with and share and enjoy things with them. When we are overburdened all the time (because of clutter), our loved ones—family members, mate, friends, boss, whomever—may accept it, but most find it uncomfortable or resent it. The space all that clutter takes up around us is not nearly as bad as the space it creates *between* us and everyone else.

Amazing, how old expressions can sum up today's problems: "Where your treasures are, there will your heart be also."

How many times have we been called upon or needed and found our junk (and our obligation to it) is so deep we can't do a thing?

The editor of one of the nation's largest newspapers brought to my attention an excellent illustration of the persecution of piles. I was escorted to the second floor of his building once to dejunk some desks (at least fifty of the eighty "workstations" in the huge room had no visible working surface left). He gestured to two of the worst: "It happens time and time again, Don. We get calls for these two fellows and report them not in, because the stuff is piled so high around them we couldn't see them at their desks."

We will all defend to the death our right to retain whatever we want, as much as we want, for as long as we want. But it isn't really my desk, my drawer, my room, my storage bin, my office. The famous phrase (used by all of us, and at least ten million teenagers a day) "It's *my* life—I can do what I want!" seems so logical and constitutionally correct, but it's not. Believe it or not, like it or not, you are not a single entity in life, but a part of society, of a family, a partnership, a community, a company, a team, a marriage. The weight in, on, and around you is carried and shared by *others*, too. Too much isn't a purely private issue—our stuff slows up lines, consumes energy and resources, and makes space too tight. This is a "we" life we have here, not a "me" life!

Claiming that your stuff is strictly your problem is like claiming that smoking, stealing, dangerous driving, or an infectious disease is your problem alone. Letting your surplus infringe on others amounts to stealing their space and time. Even making people look at your clutter all the time is unfair!

Ownership Affects Our Values

Once, I had boarded a plane—watched all of the passengers cram their things under the seats and into the overstuffed overhead bins—and then we sat as departure time came and went. The captain's voice came over the PA system: "We have a little mechanical problem with the aircraft; expect a few minutes' delay." Seconds later, the entire cabin was filled with smoke and a burning smell. I was a few rows behind First Class, and I saw several of those passengers jump from their seats in panic, fling open the bins, and wrestle to remove their oversize bags and packages. Two big fellows rescued not only their huge backpacks, but their five-foot fishing rods as well, effectively blocking the aisle, which was now filled with frantic passengers from the rest of the plane.

Others, following suit, rushed for their stuff. Several people behind me yelled, *"Leave your stupid things and get off this plane!"* The people who were plugging up our escape exit grasped their treasures and plodded off the plane, delaying more than 100 other people who could have been seriously injured or even killed. We shook our heads in disgust and disbelief that saving stuff could come before saving yourself, and for that matter, the rest of us.

The Larger Implications of Clutter

This clutter issue has bigger implications yet. Something that made a lifetime impression on me—the single thing I remember from Sociology 101 back in college—was the professor asking if we knew the single biggest problem in our worldwide society. His answer: the coexistence of starvation and plenty. Most Americans have an abundance and daily waste all manner of things while more than a billion people— fellow humans—are living in poverty on our planet. This is a sobering reality. While many of us are overfed, cluttered up, and unappreciative, a large portion of the world's population would risk their lives for our crumbs. Six million children die a year around the world from malnutrition.

> Our excess possessions squander the earth's resources. A New Yorker, for instance, uses 120 times more of the earth's resources in his or her lifetime than does an inhabitant of Madagascar, as noted in the *World Ecology Report*.

The real ugliness of having and tending "too much" is not only what it does to us individually, but the blockage it causes, the curtain it puts up so we cannot see and serve those without. We may say, "When and if I have plenty, I'll give to the needy." But "much" muffles charity, not encourages it as you might suppose.

When hurricane Iniki hit the Hawaiian island of Kauai with winds of up to 200 mph, my home (built of concrete) escaped unscathed, but the neighbors' homes didn't. Whole houses were gone, and there were miles of road with all the telephone poles down across them. Suddenly, there was no water, no phones, no television, no electricity—and this lasted for weeks and months. Stuck-up, stingy, selfish, unsociable neighbors suddenly became givers and sharers—they became friendly. It was wonderful. But as soon as the poles were all back up, and TV, phones, and good water were restored—the minute they had their much and many back—those same neighbors reverted back to unsociable and selfish. Interesting, but not surprising.

It Affects Our Kids

Abusing children in any way, physically or emotionally, or neglecting them, is, in my opinion, the only unforgivable sin on this earth. When we hear accounts of child starvation and abandonment, most of us are irate or horrified. Yet have you ever thought about "too much" as almost an equal unkind- ness to children?

Having everything is almost as abusive as having nothing. We now are burying our children with too much—too many things and opportunities.

Our children now are getting less parenting and more playthings, less personal responsibility and more pleasures. They have more machines and fewer muscles; confections are overtaking affections. Think on this a minute or two and it will give "too much" new meaning!

We ride this "Excess Express" from infancy onward . . . kids constantly asking for things, buying and getting every- thing they want, when they want it, and actually being raised up to be junkers. Look at how bad we old duffers are, and we had little, or not more than a tenth of what is available to kids today, when we were young. Yet look where we are now: clut- tered in. Just think of all that is available to newer generations, and with less discipline, too. How much junk will they have by the time they are thirty, forty, and fifty? It will be horrendous, and will affect their marriages, jobs, and self-esteem. And let's not even try to imagine what size homes and storage units they will need to contain it all, or what will be done to the earth in the process of producing all this. It's a bloated future ahead! This weekend is a good time to change the trend!

What did the most for us as children? It was having less and working more (we all testify to that). And yet, almost 100 percent of us are seeing to it that our kids work less and have more—the exact opposite of what helped to build us!

Here is a big push-over-the-edge question to ask yourself: "How is my 'too much' affecting others? Could it be irritating them, embarrassing them, taking their time and space? Even costing them?" Who are those others?

- Family/spouse
- Neighbors
- Friends
- Employers
- Future generations

So if you don't want to start decluttering this weekend for yourself, do it for those you love . . . and watch them love you—more!

The Biggest Price Tag of "Too Much"

The biggest price tag of "too much" is its blotting-out power. Clutter creates an unnoticed layer of insulation—like a callus that can render us insensitive to or unaware of what's going on around us.

The work was hard on the farm where I grew up, and our hands soon had a tough layer of calluses from handling hay bales and shovel handles. Late one evening in harvest time, we were finishing up with our combine, which had two stacks coming up out of the motor—one was a cool air stack, and the other an exhaust pipe, which was often red hot. Since it was dark and I was tired and careless, I grabbed what I thought was the air pipe to swing down from the platform—but it was the exhaust pipe. I heard my hand sizzle and saw smoke issuing from my palm. My hand looked charred, and I dreaded the thought of a permanently scarred hand. But the next morning my hand was fine—no pain, no damage. The heat of the pipe hadn't penetrated through the calluses. Luckily for me, this was an amazing testimony to how "insulation" can shield incoming messages. Often the calluses of "too much" and "too busy" keep us from feeling the fine things that are at hand.

> Your extra storage shed is on your property, not just your land, but your emotional property, crowding out your loved ones and some of your capacities to comprehend or consider all that is at hand.

Stuff—excess stuff—is the culprit that causes us to miss many of the "now" moments of life. The time to do something often comes only once. If we don't do it then, the feeling that we've lost it haunts us. It was going and now it's gone. It was right there—we were *just* about to grab it. Then we were distracted for a while (playing with or taking care of *our stuff*); it flashed by, and we missed it. It was gone, that moment to love, to say something, feel it, do it, to savor the beauty. Isn't it frustrating to see so many things to do, places to go, people to love, experiences to cherish, and you are getting little or none of all this because you are locked into the stagnation of your stuff?

The Real Price of Clutter: Life Space, Not Living Room Space!

Most of us consider the main evil of clutter to be the fact that it takes up our room—a simple matter of real estate. But that is not the prime pinch of those piles and heaps. Many of us can afford to get, or already have, the space to clutter forever. You might have four barns and ten acres, two parents' houses, and even free warehouse room to keep your collection of clutter. But be reminded that the floor space isn't the killer—it's the mental and emotional space clutter takes. Clutter crowds and smothers kindness, romance, commitment, organization, freedom, almost everything.

With clutter, we end up tending trivia, instead of our timely needs. The energy and emotion spent to carry along or climb over too much keeps pulling living into a secondary position.

If we used only a quarter of the ingenuity, resources, and rationalizing power that we use to purchase and preserve our stuff, on our health, family, job, or spirituality, we'd be way ahead.

> "You might say clutter is a way of avoiding life—you can spend your time being overwhelmed by things and working hard to get them straightened out, instead of doing something more meaningful."

Once you're free of all those piles, you can at last go after what is whistling past in life. Once you're dejunked, too, your seeds can grow. You, like any living thing, have numerous seeds (potentials, dreams, opportunities) inside you. But if there is no room for them to take root and sprout, seeds cannot and will not grow. When we're too junked, it jams our ambition and creativity. We spend our time floundering rather than in fascinating, productive, growing experiences.

And Now for the Biggest Convincer

You don't just carry clutter . . . it carries over. There is a connection between a grudge and a garage. Your garage is full of clutter, you can't seem to rid yourself of it, and it has much the same effect as a grudge you can't get rid of. Both of them punish you every single day. There is a simple, almost infallible principle here: You become what you have. Your exposure to and possession of all these things is inhaled into your entire being. All of that stuff around you doesn't just sit there innocently being too much. It silently and swiftly transfers its spirit and its weight onto you. We've all seen someone pick up a laugh, an accent, an ability, an attitude, just being around a person or a place for a while. So think of all those negatives of your stuff transferring to you. Remember the old adage, "First we criticize, then we tolerate, and then embrace" (most of the time despising what we embrace). This is called carryover, and clutter has big-time potential for carryover.

Your clutter, all that junk around you, is forming your future. You cannot stop this except by shedding all those sacks and stacks of overload . . . *right now, this very weekend!*

Why Dejunk?

To feel better. To stop feeling bogged down, disorganized, depressed, out of control.

To get more enjoyment out of life. You enjoy life a lot more when you aren't spending all that time digging in storage bins, dusting shelves, and working overtime to pay for stuff you didn't really want or need.

To be able to travel light. Clutter takes away our freedom and limits our lifestyle. We can't leave it or stop worrying about it. Clutter makes travel an ordeal rather than a pleasure.

To think more clearly. When you're buried in clutter, you have no time for yourself, and no chance to think clearly or to make forward motion on the things that *really* matter to you.

To become a master manager. It'll be so much easier to operate after you dejunk, that you'll immediately be able to get a lot more done every day. You'll be able to find things when you need them and cleaning will take half the time it did before.

For the image we give. Admit it or not, like it or not, we all have an image, and junk and clutter never create a good impression.

For better relationships. No two ways about it, clutter is unsexy, even repulsive, and it gets between us and other people.

For space. Aren't we all today, everywhere, feeling crowded, enclosed, and short of space?

To save money. Dejunked people not only tend less, they spend less.

For safety's sake. Clutter is the culprit behind many accidents, fires, injuries, and other disasters.

For aesthetics. No matter how you look at it, clutter is visual pollution. Cluttered places are ugly and unattractive.

For the carryover. Once you get the physical clutter out, you'll be amazed how fast the mental clutter follows.

Chapter 3

The Big Question: When?

(The Answer: *This Weekend!*)

There is one sure thing about clutter: It is not just going to go away by itself. It has never been known to evaporate or dissolve, and very few robbers are likely to take it. And the good fairy with the magic wand is probably at Wal-Mart buying more clutter herself. So what is yours is yours and will remain yours until you take command of it. You've had ownership of it long enough, and your chances of another Great Depression occurring to make you desperate enough to use it all, or of a traveling antique show coming into town to buy your cache, are so remote, they can't be measured. Your alternative is really the weekend—preferably this one.

When Is Bigger Than Why, What, and How

The whole force of the word "intention" hinges on when we intend to do something. We may know why, what, how, and where, but all of these ready-to-go talents and commitments are useless without a "when."

So the real question is: What can make us shed our clutter now?

Remember how stubborn we could be before saying "uncle" as kids? There was some pride or machismo that would allow another kid to twist our arm or hold our head under the drinking fountain—punish us unmercifully—and still we would not come out with that "uncle" to get relief. I can recall the biggest, heaviest kid on the block sitting on me—it actually felt like he was crushing every bone in my body. But he still couldn't get me to say "uncle."

Even as grown-ups we hate to run up the white flag, to surrender even things that are really hurting us. We don't like to admit that anyone or anything could get the best of us. So instead we let overbearing people—or our overload of clutter— push us to the breaking point. That is the crucial time when, regardless of how unyielding we are, the bone, the back, the bag, the belt, the brain, the being is going to snap from the "too much."

---

*Don't wait another minute to yell "uncle" to your excess.
You will in the end, you know, so why endure any more?*

Why do we put off getting rid of things until they start to really punish us? For sure, most of us already know:

- How much harm our clutter is doing to us
- Why we should get rid of it
- Where it should go

We already know all this, but it is the big *when* that is generally the holdback. We are even willing to admit that we are going to have to correct things, so doesn't it seem odd that we still put it off?

We could declutter ourselves at twenty, thirty, or forty years of age and be in control, confident, and comfortable for the rest of our lives. But too often we choose to keep fighting our excess for twenty or thirty years. Finally, at age sixty or seventy we decide to implement the big *when*, and we really regret all those years of "bearing the burden" and having pro-crastinated. In the end it comes down to: How fast do you want relief and freedom?

Bear in mind, too, that while you are debating and "trying to find the time" to unload yourself, more is funneling into those piles you are going to purge. The best course for all con-cerned is to get started *this* weekend. Then you'll have the rest of your weekends for things you want to do—not what your overloads let you do. After all, you've often asked yourself, "Who's in charge around here anyway?"

Everyone gets tired of their "too much"—they hate the weight of it, they hate to have it noticed and commented on, they hate facing it every time they look in their hearts or the mirror, or walk through the garage.

Doing It Now Will Avert Problems and Disasters

As the old saying goes, "You can pay me now or pay me more later." Dealing with things now gives you more choice than later and will avert many problems and even disasters.

I had a friend who was really into the sport of bow hunting, and his dedication and hours of practice turned him into an expert marksman. In one practice session, he split an arrow, rendering it worthless. Instead of trashing it as he should have, he (as we do with junk) put it back in the quiver with all the good arrows, to fix or toss out later.

Hunting with a bow rather than a gun gives you about one-tenth the opportunity to bag game, for thirty times the walking. He hunted hard the entire season, without getting anything even close to a decent shot. On the last day of hunting season, he took his bow with him on a job we were doing in Sun Valley's Sawtooth Mountains. On the way out we rounded a bend and there was a herd of deer right by the roadside, in a little clearing amidst the pines and aspens. I eased the pickup to a silent stop, and my friend, who was riding in the back with his bow, slipped out of the back of the truck. The deer still hadn't moved, and they were three times closer than the targets he regularly bull's-eyed. He loaded his bow carefully, aimed, and released the arrow. It veered wildly and sank deep into a tree ten feet from the lucky buck he was aiming at.

You guessed it! He'd pulled out the split arrow and thus undid all practice and opportunity. Saved stuff will punish us as we go along and for sure later, too. And we won't get to select the time and circumstances.

As one law officer called to an incredibly cluttered, condemned house put it, "This is a time bomb waiting to go off." A little timely attention can head off many coming explosions in life.

Think of All the Time You'll Save

In the 1960s I designed and installed landscape sprinkler systems for Sun Valley Resort, and necessarily had quite an inventory of sprinkler parts. The used and replaced parts gradually got mixed in with the new parts. I planned to sort and separate later. You know how it goes: Even though we may have time right then, it just isn't convenient. When it came time to move all this sprinkler gear to our new home in Pocatello, I just loaded it all up, lugged it home, and stuffed it all in a giant storage bin for "later." For years afterward, that big bin took up room and had to be dodged around, and I dreaded the prospect of sorting it every time I needed a good part. But I kept waiting for later.

Finally I was in the position of just plain having to go through it, so I sorted through and ended up trashing dozens of totally worthless sprinkler heads and hose connectors. It only took me thirty minutes, and yet over the preceding thirty years I'd spent at least twenty hours pawing through the mess looking for good parts that were mixed with the bad. Later is such a waste of efficiency and life!

Declutter this weekend! The sooner you do it, the more time you'll save. One of my readers pointed out, for example, that the quarterly reports she had to do for her business always took 2½ days . . . for years. Then she thinned out the papers in her office, dumped the excess and unneeded from files and desks and the like—she got rid of the junk. Those reports now take less than a day. If she did quarterly reports four times a year for the next thirty years of her business, that would mean 200 hours—five whole workweeks—of free or reclaimed time. Just for removing a bit of excess. If we decluttered a dozen other time and space takers, the time saved and quality of life gained would be almost immeasurable. We could gain two or three whole years of pure free time. That should be enough to make us launch into our excesses this weekend!

When Is the Perfect Time to Do It?

There will never be a perfect moment or a naturally occurring vacant weekend to dive into those clutter caches. We all have plenty—in fact far too much—to do these days. We have dozens—maybe even hundreds—of plans and projects, things to fix, things to check out, things to take care of, books to read, books to write, things to invent, visits to make, trips to take. Right now your brain is swimming with want-to's, need-to's, and should-do's. In the reality of everyday life—making a living, taking care of the house and yard, tending our mate, keeping up with the kids, keeping well, and being at least a little bit spiritual—getting down to doing something about that "too much" may seem almost impossible.

But if we wait until every other life pursuit is attended to before we proceed with dejunking, if we stop for every little setback or interruption, the big *when* will never come. You don't have to stop living to put your life in order—you can do it even if your life is in a shambles. In fact, often the best time to rid yourself of what is hurting you is *when* you are hurting. A big secret of the phenomenal people you know is they generally make their whens *now*, this weekend, this evening, this year. "Sometime" is too often lost in time, and as fast as life is going by, it may well be never.

> Can you name a time in life when you need extra baggage?
> Dropping it off and keeping it off is not something to
> do later in life "when all the busy-ness has died down."
> The time to do it is now, during the busy time.

Forget "the Ledge"

Often we put off dejunking or push it ahead, telling ourselves that someday a "ledge" will appear that will enable us to do it. What is that elusive ledge? You and I both have tucked away in our minds a "place" somewhere between hope and desperation. For me, it's a niche, a space, a time out, where I can step off the merry-go-round and rest a while to process everything.

Where I can catch up and get ahead, and then step back into the routine of life and get on with it. All my life I've looked forward to getting to that ledge, that nook I could duck into for a week or month or whatever and tear into all those overdue things. Like maybe when I break a leg and am laid up, or when a new machine comes along to speed things up. Believe it or not, whenever I see a prison movie, I always think, "Man, if I were ever imprisoned for a while, could I catch up!"

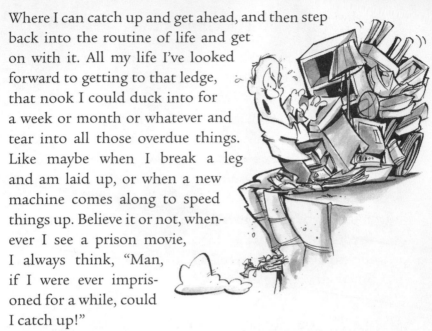

Well folks, I've been waiting for at least fifty years now, and that ledge has never appeared. I have a big family and many employees and several companies of my own that you'd think might be a help here, but that ledge to duck out of the line of fire for a few days has never appeared. In fact, just the opposite has happened. The longer I live and the more independent, secure, in control, and responsible I get, the more I have to do. I'm getting busier all the time with bigger and better things.

The only answer is *now*. Today you have the time and ways and means to declutter. Start with what is around you first, and watch how much relief and carryover comes to the "too much" in your head and on your body.

NOW is the time—you've already tried waiting and that hasn't worked or lessened the weight. Time doesn't heal clutter, it only multiplies it!

Maybe . . . (Just Maybe) It Will Go Away

We are all idealistic enough to nurture the vision, however unlikely, that a miracle might happen, and tomorrow morning we will wake up to find our whole place gleaming, with no junk at all. We're dreaming, of course, but it would be nice, and even the thought of it offers some relief and comfort. More realistically, we may think we are getting away with it, because no one has said anything to us about our clutter recently. Or our junk is buried so deep in mind or under the mattress that it isn't bugging us right now—plus we are building a bigger garage.

If you are still waiting for a miracle on your street and in your storage bin, the wait will be longer and more unrewarding than you can imagine.

Maybe I Can Get Away from It All

Once you leave your home with all its excesses, you arrive at your vacation destination and the same "all" is there: boutiques, shops, stands, high prices, crowds, souvenirs and more souvenirs, exotic and local junk, and stuff of all kinds. One can hardly 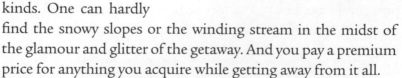 find the snowy slopes or the winding stream in the midst of the glamour and glitter of the getaway. And you pay a premium price for anything you acquire while getting away from it all.

It's amazing how many people think of moving (to a new house or location) as an anticipated solution for excess stuff. Don't count on it—the average packrat can have it all back in a matter of months.

Perhaps a Letup as I Age—Right?

Given the experience of the years you have already lived with "it," how would you bet? Everything that contributes to the overload around us is only going to increase to runaway proportions from here. Most of us are well beyond having everything we really need, and still we are offered hourly an ever-widening selection of stuff on every side. Day by day there will be only more and better things to buy, and it will be easier to do so.

In the past decade, the number of places offering us new goodies has at least doubled, between mail-order companies, specialty stores, magazines, and Web sites. Before long there will probably be thousands more television channels and most of them will be cooking, shopping, and infomercial networks—providing us with everything and more in the blink of a screen. Just about everything today can be gotten quickly and easily, and the amount of home space per person has never been greater. All this availability and convenience and all this room only coaxes us into more. No way are any of these clutter sources going to wither away and die.

If you are waiting for the weight to let up, you are going to be let down. The "times" are not suddenly going to release and relieve you, because more—much more—is coming to add to your overload. Clutter doesn't retire when you do—it grows by itself.

Count on it, more is coming and it will double and triple your tonnage. Can you imagine your home's condition after a few more years of gaining pound upon pound every day? Your present ownership speaks for you, and it says, "You'll take more." The amount of junk you have now is just a hint of the *more* you are going to accumulate.

"I'm Going to Do It Later"

This illusion of "later" is a liar that tells us we have plenty of time left. We don't! When it comes to our mortal time here on earth, reality is counted in decades. Note the evolution here.

From age one to twelve, a lifetime is forever.

From twelve to eighteen, we can tell it is moving.

From eighteen to thirty-five, it picks up speed.

From thirty-five to sixty, a flash!

At age sixty, we could be gone in the twinkling of an eye, any time now.

In reviewing my agenda for the years ahead a while ago, I suffered a real shock when I divided my remaining time into weeks. Weeks really whiz by for most of us, don't they? Before we know it, it's Monday again. I'm seventy now, and if I live until eighty, I have only 520 weeks left to fulfill my intentions. That's scary—not necessarily the fact of being gone, but the thought of all the things I still want to do that may never get done, the prospect of not accomplishing as much as I wanted of the lifetime of expectations I've been accumulating. Our physical accumulation, junk and clutter, is one big blocker of those special things you really want to get done. How much longer do you intend to let it linger in the way?

> "Upon dejunking, I found many unsent greeting cards that were yellowed, or gifts 'to give someday' that were now ruined or outdated."

The Crater of Later

Clutter doesn't get any better with time. It breeds and multiplies, simply by being stored, tended, thought about, and talked about. Any plans to lose it later are just promises for its proliferation. Later digs a bigger crater to fill, and then you inevitably will have to face it in the future, a future in which you will be much busier than you are now. You have more time right now than you ever will have. Just ask any retired person who lived for the day of "no more work" so he could finally get around to everything else he wanted to do. He will testify that he can't figure out how he ever had time to work and raise a family because he is so terribly busy now.

When you feel a strong desire to simplify your life, don't let it slip past until the deadly "later." Ignoring it for "just a little longer" is just setting yourself up for a slow strangulation of your time, space, and emotions.

Junk and clutter just sour by the hour. Waiting just causes things to date, date, date. Each day there is more punishment and less value.

Talk about an argument against "later"--listen to what one New Jersey woman had to say:

"In the bottom of the box, I found a small gold-plated cross about one-inch square. It was given to me when I was six years old for good conduct in catechism class. My mom had put the cross away because 'it would mean more to me when I was older.' I pulled it out, grabbed a needle-nose pliers, and attached it to a bracelet, which I wore to church that day. I was so sorry I hadn't pulled it out decades ago."

Don't Dump the Job on the Next Generation

My editor made a comment that really hit me. "Isn't it a shame," she said, "that we have to die to get dejunked?" (by someone else, who has to go through it all and face the enormous physical and emotional job of sorting and deciding what to do with our stuff).

How is it possible, intelligent as we are and loving our families as we do, that we have no time in this long span of life to control our own possessions? We often have to die first to finally get it done, and then it doesn't benefit us a bit and is a real burden on others; in fact, it's nothing less than a curse to them. We almost cannot leave enough money or property to a friend or family member to compensate them for a large burden of clutter left behind. How sad that dejunking does not become a priority until we have passed on!

None of us plan on leaving the earth until we schedule it and square away everything, of course . . . when? Someday? Later? On our deathbed? The best time is now. Wouldn't it be better to get your house in order today, and have thirty, forty, or even fifty years left to enjoy freedom? If you have any love or respect for your loved ones, don't ask, expect, or force them to go through your stuff after you're gone. A lifetime of your good deeds can be blotted out by the one bad deed of expecting others to deal with your "estate" (composed of assorted "too much").

Our heirs shouldn't have to face and fight our failure to deal with our own assets or liabilities, shouldn't have to discover some of the very personal things they are going to find, going through all that.

Today is the day to make the resolution, "I will not leave all this for my family to deal with when I'm gone." Deal with it now—this weekend! Don't give anyone the opportunity to hate you for your junk. Don't make them lug your legacy around!

Substitute "Today" for "Someday"

SOMEDAY. You can use this expression as one word, "someday," or two words, "some day," and you can be sure that the bigger the space between the "some" and the "day," the more stuff will be in the way. The longer you wait, the more crowds in between the "some" and the "day," the farther they get separated, and the more likely that *someday will never come.*

You can't take it with you! Anyone counting on that "big attic in the sky" needs to quit counting, it won't be there. Remember, it's dust to dust, ashes to ashes, clutter to parents' or children's place, heaven help us.

In our dialogues and conversations through life, what would happen if we were to substitute the word "today" for "someday"? Imagine the impact—wow! Do this with your clutter and it will carry over into your relationships and other parts of your life. The other somedays of your life ("someday I'll write," "someday I'll visit," "someday I'll read," "someday I'll have that looked at," "someday I'll change") will be directly influenced by the someday of your junk and clutter.

Why would you want to live with and around all of that unnecessary stuff any longer? I ask you this, others are asking you (silently perhaps), and when you start asking yourself, you are on the way to the makeover weekend!

Why Not Go for the Quick Cure?

Why let the piles of the past or present oppress what time is left—be it months or decades? When is a better time than now to put the problems and burdens of the past behind you?

After years of suffering from the discomfort of headaches, insomnia, back pain, arthritis, ringing in the ears, or whatever, what if someone offered you relief that involved no cost and no drugs—just a weekend of simple activities and it would all go away? How would you react? There's no doubt about it—you wouldn't wait a minute to eliminate those nagging, punishing plagues. Why not do the same for that which is suffocating, distracting, and burdening you—the weight on, in, and around you, your stuff, that ugly EXCESS!

Attack the source! So many people try to handle continual stress or trauma through drugs, special exercises, and counseling—things that seldom cure it, just reduce it to a level that's tolerable to live with. It's so much simpler just to cut the source! Why not simply stop doing the thing that is causing the pain and grief in your life? Instead, we get insulated coveralls so we can jump back into the fire, we make bigger and better storage units, and we come up with fancier names for the problem and more effective "hiding" apparel, so that we can continue to indulge in the very thing that is plunging us into depression. "No," "stop," "don't," "quit," and "declutter" are simple cure words.

How Long Are You Going to Wait to Change Things?

I get hundreds of "horror" letters from people about the pressures clutter has inflicted on them. Among the most shocking are the newspaper stories sent to me about such things. In 2004 the Everett, Washington, *Herald*, for example, carried a story about a senior citizen who died in a fire in his junk-filled home. Firefighters had trouble finding him amidst a floor-to-ceiling collection of newspapers, boxes, plastic bags, papers, old televisions, and broken furniture. Firefighters tried to break in via the basement door, but the basement was crammed full to the ceiling. Neighbors reported that when the owner was alive, there was little room to walk anywhere inside the house, and he could barely open the door when someone came to visit. We may think that dying in such circumstances would be shameful, but many of us are living in the same basic condition—our clutter just hasn't totally engulfed us yet. We are buried alive, and this is just as bad, or even worse. When is the big question here—when are we going to change things? When they find our feet sticking out from under our pile of millennium collectibles and outdated computer gear?

Don't Wait Until Junk and Clutter Are Terminal

Clutter doesn't seem to worry us too much as long as we know we have the physical strength and space to handle it. As long as we're convinced we have the upper hand, the zero hour for dejunking can come at any time. But one day we may realize that we are getting older and the junk deeper. It's become like a noxious weed out of control; we just can't hack it out now, it's gained on us. We can't even lift it now, and the friends and relatives we were going to share it with (or dump it on) are fewer and feebler.

Don't wait until you're too weak to win the war on your whatnot collection, until it has the upper hand because your hands have slowed down.

One Last Big Reason Not to Wait

If this wouldn't make you do it now, what would?

> *Dear Don,*
> *Please send my mother any hints you have on how to clear up clutter. She is a genuine packrat and our house is so cluttered I can't have my friends over. I try to help her clean the house but I don't know where to start. I am twelve years old and would like to have my friends over . . . sometime.*

Believe it or not, folks, I get letters like this from kids all the time. Might your children be being cheated out of life too, because you are choosing to live with stuff that crowds them out? If you can't or won't dejunk for yourself, do it for your children. Your overfull rooms will educate them more effectively than any classroom—in all the wrong things.

"But . . ." But What?

Here come the excuses, and we've heard them all, from "As soon as I toss it, I'll need it" to "It was a gift. . . ." "It's handmade . . . ," "It's the last one . . . ," and "I'll find its mate, someday . . . ." I have no end of good excuses for clutter on file, and there are some amazing ones among them.

From the guy who kept a big box full of combination locks to which he had no combination:

"My mother-in-law is a chronic junker. The next time we go to visit her, I'm going to bring along that box of old locks, and tell her I am going to dump them because I can't find the combination. I can just see her now, spinning those dials frantically in hopes of lucking on to the combination and saving them from extinction. Oh, sweet revenge."

From the woman who has a badly warped wood trivet that has ruined ten tabletops:

"Well, I might have a warped pan I need to take to the table someday."

From the man who saves dead batteries:

"When I get mad at my wife, I go down to the basement and crush them in my vise."

Well maybe, once in a while, an excuse is justified. But the percentages are against you.

The number-one excuse for keeping an overkill of stuff, too much, is "I might need it someday." If you wait long enough (like eighty years), that might be an entirely true statement, but what about in the meantime? Even the valuable has a devaluation point, when it crowds and crazes your existence too much right now.

Like that old motor you hung on to. You kept it and kept it, and it stained the garage floor and skinned your shanks more than once when you stumbled over it. Years later, when a use finally came, you had to upgrade that motor's emissions and the total cost was $30 more than just buying a new one.

Or that cast-iron cookstove, "just like Grandma used to use," you bought at a real bargain price and dreamed of installing in a rustic cabin in the woods someday. Meanwhile, it took up about a quarter of the garage, dented one car door and a fender, and provided a great place for messy families of mice to nest. You had to pay four strong men to help out every time it had to be moved for any reason. By the time you were actually in a position to consider a cabin in the woods, the stove was so badly rusted no fire would dare be made in it, and one leg had given way.

Even if you do use something, keeping it might not pay. A man bought a $170 machine. He kept it for twenty years and used it only once every five. All that time he stored it, people asked to borrow it. He could have rented the same machine for $10 when he needed it, and would have paid a total of only $40 rent over all that time. Plus he wouldn't have had to store it, maintain it, try to retrieve it from the people who borrowed it, and so on.

What about that big pile of old shingles you kept, insisting they might come in handy someday? For more than two decades, the pile took up the space in the shed you really could have used to keep the mower out of the rain and sun. All that time, the pile looked ugly and gave rats and snakes a place to hide. A possible use for the shingles finally surfaces, but you can't use them because you've discovered they're full of asbestos. You can't even find a place to get rid of them now, because no landfill or garbage pickup service wants them.

Some Simple Math Will Show the Way

It's time to play the percentages. Interesting how basic the answers to many problems are, and this "too much" problem comes down to simple arithmetic. If you understand addition, subtraction, multiplication, and division, you have your problem figured out. As long as you continue with addition (buying and getting more and bringing it home), you will end up with more. With clutter, you don't have to know how to multiply because junk is self-perpetuating—one thing needs another, a matching one, a shelf, an accessory, something to complement it or contrast with it, a tool or two to tend it— and soon what you have added has been multiplied. If you try division—splitting or dividing junk (especially with kids and friends)—you will usually end up with the remainder.

Simple math leaves you only one logical alternative: . . . subtraction. Now that works—you have five, subtract three, and you have two, along with more room, more peace, etc. There is no mystery as to what relieves us; it's taking away, subtraction, and the only time is *this weekend*!

What you need to do with those excess objects of all kinds is to shed them—and I don't mean move them to the backyard shed either. The "shed" I'm referring to here means to get rid of, evict, discard, eliminate, chuck, ditch, dump, reject, recycle, or scrap them.

"But My Clutter Problem Is Serious"

Let's not let this undertaking get too complicated. Sometimes a simple problem is made complicated in the solving.

Many people with a clutter problem seek an exotic diagnosis for it, and then go off for counseling, hire a professional dejunker, visit a clinic, join a club, make a public or private confession of it, or file clutter-uptcy. We can go off the deep end finding all kinds of genetic and deep psychological reasons for "our problem" when it isn't necessary. We may not have a serious case of compulsive packrat-ism. We may have simply picked up and stored too much—totally normal conduct in our incredibly "over-offered" world. You don't have to consider institutionalizing yourself over too many shoes or cardboard boxes (with who-knows-what in them). We aren't usually dealing with a pathological problem here—decluttering is a form of cleaning, something we all understand and can do.

Seldom do we need support. We just need a little simple deporting of things. We need to spend less time worrying about the difference between our right and left brain, and just use our whole brain to clear out the clutter and free ourselves. And when we walk away from the excess stuff around us, many of our other problems will walk away from us.

Own Up to Your Clutter

Until we quit blaming other people for unloading it on us, or coming forth with "no time" as the reason we're not getting rid of our clutter, we aren't going to get anywhere.

> Getting rid of something you just don't want anymore
> is taking control, the ultimate act of ownership!

I've noticed a parallel to chronic junkers in parents whose kids end up in serious problems. Many a parent's main rationale for a child's problems is "he/she got in with the wrong crowd." It's never the kid's fault; it's always the "wrong crowd" that caused the heartaches. (Note the crowd never gets any credit when the kid exceeds everyone's expectations.) As long as your clutter problem is your spouse, your too-small house, the parent who gave it all to you, the company that keeps sending you catalogs, and so on, you'll never get anywhere with your stuff. Ownership is one thing, but taking *full* ownership is the key to conquering clutter. Once the tattered toy duck stops here, you're on your way!

You Can Lose It!

Fortunately, to fix things here there is nothing you have to buy or join. You just need to do a little shakedown of some of that "too much" you're sick and tired of having around anyway. The great day of dejunking takes no skill or money—just a bit of deciding, digging, and doing. Instant results this weekend!

Try a Space Lift Instead of a Face Lift!

The miracles of modern surgery can offer us all kinds of cosmetic operations and procedures. And surely there is a time and place when a "face lift" might be truly beneficial, to remove sagging or excess skin and erase bumps, bulges, and blemishes. But think of the "doctoring" you and I could do ourselves to make us feel better and make us more attractive, by giving a place lift or space lift to all of that sagging and nagging stuff around us! We have the time, the place, and the credentials to do it; after all, we own all of it. A weekend spent dejunking will beat a two-day self-esteem seminar any day—just try it!

What a Wonderful Anti-Aging Agent!

If Ponce De Leon had pounced on his extra stuff instead of searching for the fountain of youth, he would have been a good part of his life ahead. We can't do much about the process of aging, but we can stop doing things that speed up the process. Think for a minute: What has put the most miles on your body and soul? Acquiring, organizing, sorting, shuffling, and retrieving stuff! All of that dragging, lifting, stashing, and unstashing are what wear you down and out.

How Long Will It Take?

These are the days of instant gratification—fast foods, push-button entertainment, nonstop flights, speedy oil changes, instant answers, one-hour photos, next-day delivery, quick-drying paint. We are almost back to the childhood stage of wanting and expecting everything immediately—patience, investment, saving, and waiting are hardly even part of our thinking process anymore. All of us are getting this way, so don't think you are excused from wanting results right now, not ten years from now:

- "How fast does it grow?"
- "How soon will this pill work?"
- "When will that package get there?"
- "Fax it, please."

We all insist on speed several times every day, and in response to this, things are faster, almost unbelievably so. Mail that once took months can now be transmitted in minutes, even from overseas! In seconds, we can do mathematical and engineering calculations that took even brilliant people days before.

Yet when it comes to our clutter, this is one time our estimates of how long it will take to do something (get *rid* of it) go into centuries. But all those piles and heaps, closets and cabinets full! It'll take months, maybe years, to even make a dent in this.

Not so! There is fast disposal, too, and really the only slow part—the part you have to be concerned with—is your commitment to do it. People will be out to your house or lawn almost instantly when you put out the word or the sign that you are going to give some of your stuff away. One weekend will get you a long way.

Remember:

It always comes back to your personal decision.

It is going to be a bigger courtyard or less clutter.

It is going to be a bigger headache or more headroom.

You have to choose. You can use your time to fight stuff or to forge ahead. Freedom is as close as your calendar, so let's get started . . . this weekend!

Chapter 4
The Power of a Weekend

A magazine I was writing an article for once sent me a report on our growing weekend mentality. It explained (complete with facts and figures) how Americans were thinking more and more in terms of weekends—looking forward to and planning for each weekend eagerly as it approaches. Weekend getaways are more important than ever as stress and job pressures mount in our lives. This made me more aware of weekends than I'd ever been before. Having been raised on a farm, and a self-employed entrepreneur all my life, I'd always viewed weeks as a steady stretch of seven days—I never separated the weekend out. But to most people who work a regular nine-to-five job for someone else, the weekend is a precious, almost sacred thing—"my time," or "our time," at last!

This is why the weekend is the perfect time for a full-fledged decluttering campaign. It's the perfect time to un-accumulate, though most of us don't use it that way. Mostly, weekends are spent seeking and acquiring more. So let's make a big switch here. Let's give the weekend a whole different approach. Besides, some of those other weekend activities are getting old—going to the same old parties, games, and entertainments; having the same old conversations; spending too much money; and fighting the pounds we acquire from the usual weekend traditions. Taking one weekend and using it to *restore* instead of add more might just be the most exciting thing you've done in years.

In the next few chapters, you'll find detailed guidance on the actual process of decluttering. This chapter will just give you a brief overview.

Prime Yourself and Do Some Prospecting

You do want to do a little preparation before launching into your weekend dejunking activities. Make the first four days of the week—Monday through Thursday—observation and reconnaissance missions. As you go about your everyday activities, take a realistic look around and do some sizing up of all the things you'd like to be rid of. Then make a mental note or a written list of the things that bother you the most. You're doing all of this to prepare your agenda and set a mood.

Then, clear the weekend. Cancel, call off, or forget about the usual siege of sitting half-asleep in front of the television or racing around all over. Shut off the TV, the cell phone, the e-mail, the noise. Except for possibly one carefully chosen helper (see Chapter 5), work to be alone for the weekend. Send the family away and tell people you are away, hang blankets over the windows, and leave the newspaper out. Nothing is worse, when you are raring to go get the unnecessary out of your life and home, than to have someone interrupt your mood or method with some trivia or idle conversation. Alone one weekend, just you and your stuff, will be the ultimate getaway weekend. Another reason to be alone while you declutter is that you won't have anyone trying to convince you to keep things you've finally decided to get rid of, which means you can divest yourself of dumb gifts or silly souvenirs people may have given you over the years without hurting anyone's feelings.

Let's break the big weekend into three parts now.

Friday

Friday has always been the kickoff day for weekend warrior activities, and by Friday, you will have decided whether you are going to do a "subject sort"(concentrate on one type of clutter that really bugs you, wherever it may be), a whole-house purge, or a room-by-room rescue.

As soon as you get home from work (or all day Friday, if you happen to be lucky enough to be off), *reveal!* Tear out, get out, spread out, unpack, dig out, and pour out all the things you need to deal with. . . . Well, maybe not all, but whatever you've decided needs to be cleaned out of your life and home *now*. See Chapters 6 and 7 if you need some help with your scouting sessions. As you pull out the clutter, instantly trash anything that is obviously junk. Once you start, you will be much more ruthless than you thought you'd be, especially when you see how awful some of the stuff is. By the time you hit the sack, you will have a commitment with little opportunity to reneg and a great Saturday to look forward to.

Saturday

Saturday is *resolve* day—when you actually go through all those piles and make the cut, trash things, ship or give them away, cull them, condense them, or otherwise dispose of them somehow. The "what" and "how" is strictly your call—you've got to be the master of all this matter you either collected yourself or otherwise have responsibility for. To help yourself out here, I would make and post a sign in some conspicuous place:

> *Does this, will this enhance my life*
> *or the lives of others?*

Eat light and healthy all this weekend—might as well reduce everything while you are on a roll. This is a good time, too, to toss some of the junk foods, sauces, and unhealthy drinks you might be tempted to indulge in later in a weak moment. With the tangible excess finally starting to move out of your life, you can let your mind review and release some of the ill feelings such as anger you may have toward others. There is something mystical about the way tossing tangibles seems to give you reasons and resolution to toss some intangibles at the same time.

Be sure to keep a pen and notepad handy throughout this whole process because a thousand thoughts, memories, ideas, to do's, and other things will pop into your head while you are decluttering. Having to stop and find something to write on may break your momentum. During all of this, you can also be playing some of those dusty CDs and tapes that are stacked everywhere—if only to see whether you really do want to keep them around.

By late Saturday night, the mess should be reduced, and all of your weed-outs either in the trash or neatly stacked in a single area from which they can be conveniently transported to Goodwill or wherever else they need to go.

Sunday

Since this is a special and often spiritual day of the week, use Sunday to refine. This means, for example, sending some of the good stuff you no longer want or need to someone who would appreciate it. Sunday is also a good day to condense and file papers, or make a scrapbook from all the little treasures you unearthed during the Friday reveal and the

Saturday resolve. It's an excellent day to continue reducing your library of reading material—books and magazines—and clear out some of the clutter on your computer.

Sunday is a great day to dig through all of the "I wonder what's in this" piles and to open all the old files and folders. Many mysteries will be solved, many small burdens will be lifted, and a new life with more freedom will come. You will find many things you thought you had lost—including genius you forgot you had long ago, and the idealism you wrote off over time so it wouldn't hurt (and you know better how to put it into action now).

Let me give you a concise summary of all the great religious writings to help inspire you. All of the advice and wisdom over the ages for getting to the root of our problems, so that we can be happy and avoid heartache and disappointment, can be summed up in three simple words: DEJUNK YOUR LIFE. Think about that. You'll find it woven into just about every sermon and spiritual directive, and in secular philosophy as well.

By the end of this weekend, you will be in a much better position to spend future weekends doing the things you really want to do—enjoying your family and friends in a neat, orderly, and comforting home, and doing things that build and enrich you.

Where Can You Find More Time to Finish?

If you aren't able to come to terms with all of your clutter in just one weekend, where can you find the time to finish?

We all feel short of time and pressed by priorities. But if we take a hard look at our daily and weekly schedule, we will probably find that some of the activities so tightly squeezed in there don't really count for much: those thirty hours of television a week, analyzing the NFL lineup or plotline of our favorite shows for two hours, and much of the stuff we are reading or running to. Many of these things just drift into our lives like all that stuff did, and they do not advance any worth-while cause. How many times have you missed something that you planned to do, and were all shaken up and irritated about it? Yet later, you realized that you really didn't miss anything at all—you were actually glad you missed it!

Let's look at the time you have available for dejunking—it's more than you think.

Take Some of Your Junk-Tending Time

That very same person—you—who just said you had no time to dejunk does somehow oddly have the time—endless time, it seems—to dust, stack, arrange, rearrange, move, and anguish over your junk. Not to mention all those expeditions you take to get more. Put a moratorium on junk tending and junk hunting for a while, till your dejunking is done. Spend those evenings and weekends purging closets and bins instead of reshuffling clutter and cruising the mall. And it'll save money, too.

Holidays

A sacrilege to even suggest dejunking on a holiday? Not really. These precious breaks from our workday routine are meant to stimulate, refresh, and uplift us. But much, if not most, of what we ordinarily do on "special days" and holidays is couch-potato, cruise around, fight crowds, and complicate our lives in noisy, expensive places. It ends up too much and we end up exhausted, aggravated, and "hung over" in more ways than one. A good solid session of dejunking, on the other hand, is one of the best drug-free highs and cures for depression around.

Independence Day—what a day to free yourself from junk!

Plan a Junk-Free Vacation

Take the time off from work, but don't go anywhere; stay home and dejunk. This stay-home dejunking vacation will end up being the finest of your life—the first real vacation you've ever had. You'll probably be $5,000 to the good, too, between what you make selling things you don't care about anymore and what you save in gas, plane fares, hotels, and not going out and about buying things.

Whenever You're Weather Bound

For most of us, at least three-quarters of our clutter is indoor clutter, so we can go after it when other activities have been wiped from the calendar by rain, snow, mud, or flood.

When there is a sudden change in our schedule or a big hunk of unexpected "downtime," we too often seem like people in jail: captured, confused, and with no way to escape. Remember that those who escape—1 out of 1,000—are the ones who use "the time" to start digging (in this case, in their clutter).

Time Fragments

Our days always have little stretches of fifteen minutes here, ten minutes here, and twenty-five minutes there when we have no choice but to wait around for something. You don't have to just twiddle your thumbs or cuss the cause of the delay—you can open a drawer (or your briefcase, or a file, or the glove compartment) and do some dejunking. We're all looking for more time, and those time fragments add up—often to most of a day. *Use them!* Clutter came in little by little, and it can go out that way, too.

The way steady daily progress adds up is like watching a tiny drip of water fill a barrel . . . overnight! A couple of culls a day is 700 pieces of clutter gone by this time next year.

You Can MAKE the Time

I know we often think we have no time to take on a single thing more in our loaded life. But if you want to dejunk badly enough, you can and will *make* the time to do it. (Just like you make the time to see someone you really want to see, or do anything you really want to do.) When we say we're "too busy" to do something, it usually means only that there are other things we want to do more. Once you truly commit and decide to declutter, you will have the time.

Chapter 5

The ABC's of Decluttering

Exactly how do you go about the process of decluttering? The process is surprisingly simple. This chapter will outline step-by-step what you need to do to unbury yourself and free both your premises and your mind from clutter.

Chart Your Course First

Big piles of junk, like a big journey, can be forbidding if you try to tackle them all at once. Before mariners set out across an ocean, they break the journey down to a "charted course." Likewise, taking that huge looming mass of clutter out of your mind and putting it on paper somehow transforms it from dreadful to doable. So if you feel the need, make a list of where and what the junk harbors are before you start, and then sort and separate your attack into some kind of order. Even if you don't follow that exact order once you begin, this exercise will trim back the intimidation and give you a sense of purpose and an overall agenda.

Here is one determined dejunker's plan:

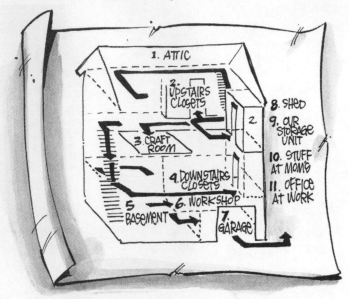

Making a plan takes only a few minutes but it gives you the big picture and a good choice of places to start. And once even a little area is conquered, it will give you that all-important *momentum*.

Stay Flexible

You do want to have an overall dejunking plan, but do stay flexible, too, because mood is one of your most important allies in dejunking. If you're walking by the woodshed and the sight of all those old cardboard boxes piled out there finally stirs you to action, forget the living room sift-through you had on today's agenda and go for the shed. If you're suddenly sick and tired of having no workspace on the kitchen counter, stop right now and make some. When it comes to clutter, mood can move mountains (and in half the time). Most clutter was attained on the spur of the moment. Maybe that's the right timetable to toss it!

Keep your master list or chart of dejunking targets and objectives posted and up to date and review it regularly. This will give you a sense of direction and control and a way of "keeping score"—you know where you're going and what you intend to do, so even if there are unexpected delays or complications, you won't get discouraged. And just wait until you start that exciting business of marking things off because they're DONE!

Get Ready for the Sorting Process

Before you start, make sure you have an easy-to-reach-and-use set of containers to put things in. These can be boxes, bags, big plastic containers, or plastic garbage cans. Nothing will delay or waylay you and break your rhythm and objectivity like having to go through things again or pick over them after you've winnowed them out once. After you've decided what their fate should be, don't dump things on the floor or pile them to "pick up later." A second handling might give something a second wind or a second chance. You want to be able to toss things right into a ready-to-go container. Here are some possibilities for your sorting categories:

1. Trash or burn
2. Recycle
3. Put back where it belongs
4. Things worth putting in storage
5. Give to the kids
6. Charity (Goodwill or the like)

Your Surgeon's Kit for Shearing Through Clutter

You want to have your clutter-cutting kit ready ahead, too. You probably won't need all of this, but here's a checklist of gear to consider. Tailor your own kit to the kind of junkscape you have to work your way through. Keep dejunking tools with you so you can snip, rip, and strip as needed.

Knife and scissors—for cutting things open and miniaturizing, see page 128.

Sturdy stepstool or stepladder—for reaching the upper shelves and top boxes. Forget about the idea of standing on any of that old junk out there instead!

Hand truck—if you have a lot of furniture and heavyweight stuff to move.

Work gloves—if you'll be handling a lot of heavy-duty or exterior things, or anything sharp, rough, or dirty. A pair of leather or other sturdy work gloves will be well worth having.

Permanent marker, labels, packing tape, and plastic storage containers and/or some of those better boxes from your box stash—for repackaging good stuff, or for discards to be sent somewhere.

Your biggest garbage cans and some good strong garbage bags—for sharp or heavy trash, a garbage box is better than a bag.

Lambswool duster, canister or wet/dry vac, dustcloth, broom, counter brush, and spray bottles of all-purpose, disinfectant, and glass cleaner—for the cleanup that always has to be done as you're clearing out.

Dust mask—if you'll be working in ultra-dusty or dirty places, a dust mask might be a good idea, especially if you're allergy prone.

Paper and pencil—for all those great ideas that always come to you when you're dejunking.

Will Having a Helper Really Help?

Some people like company when they're dejunking. I don't recommend it. One person can decide; two will debate. One is quiet progress; with more than one, you'll spend most of the time explaining or  reminiscing. To me, the biggest value in getting help here is that your helper is likely to snap up and carry off much of what you dejunk!

If you are the type who works better with a buddy, bear in mind that not just anyone will do. To aid with the delicate business of decluttering, you ideally want a helper with the following qualifications:

- Someone who knows you well enough to understand your idiosyncrasies and enthusiasms, as well as the realities of your present situation. There is no such thing as general advice about junk, only advice suited to a particular person.
- Someone sympathetic, yet practical.
- Someone whose judgment in general you respect—a winner in life.
- Someone who is less "clingy" than you when it comes to things.
- Someone you won't be embarrassed to bare your most cluttered closet or attic to.
- Someone who is capable of sticking to a project and not getting distracted (or, for that matter, distracting you).
- Someone who can keep his or her mouth shut!

Exactly *what* can this other person or persons do to truly help you out? He or she can:

- Fetch and carry things you need.
- Return or dispose of things.
- Take care of cleanup detail.
- Take care of the kids while you dejunk.
- Lend encouragement and moral support.
- Serve as "dumpster's advocate" whenever necessary.
- Help when you need a tiebreaker in the judging process—or even just serve as a sounding board for your own thinking process.
- Dejunk on his or her own some area or collection you're beyond caring about anymore, such as all that old stuff in the corner of the yard.

Your helper(s) can also help celebrate when you're done!

A good friend of mine, Dave, was helping a friend move and—as all of us who have friends with packrat proclivities know—this was no one-trip job. After they'd loaded the friend's farm truck up and sent him off to his new home with a load of stuff, there was no one left but Dave and his truck, which had a sixteen-foot bed and side boards. Dave loaded the thing completely full with junk: flat bike tires, crushed baskets, stacks of ten-year-old newspapers, broken lamps, and old faucet parts. He quickly took the entire load to the junkyard instead of the new home and dumped it. Then he hustled back and was loading the better stuff when the friend returned. The friend never missed one single item and to this day doesn't have a clue that half a semi load of his "too much" is gone.

Many of you reading this (who are quickly recounting recent moves and wondering if a "Dave" helped or not) could do the same service for yourself, much to your benefit. And there will be no regrets or misgivings, because *you* will be the picker and sorter.

Let's Get Started Now

Ready . . .
> (The junk is ready to go)

Set . . .
> (You are charted)

GO!
> (Get going, and it will go!)

As noted earlier, starting is often the hardest part of decluttering. The jump from thinking about clutter to trashing it is like the first step in anything—you'll feel strange, unsure, even awkward. But in minutes you'll be in stride, and soon you'll be sprinting.

Where to Get Started

Any place that will give a quick payoff. Somewhere (such as the shed out back or a damp, leaky cellar) where the junk is so awful, so old, so deteriorated and impersonal that you can clear away jumbo garbage cans of it in no time, without a pang of regret or a backward glance. The older a stash, the more quickly it can be cleared—our illusions about most of that stuff have aged, too.

Any place that's easy. This usually means things to which you have no emotional attachment, such as that stash of corroded cleaning supplies under the kitchen sink. Or that stuff other people left behind—it's high time to pack it up and send it back to them.

That sore spot. That place that got you into all this—the one that bugs and disgusts and impedes you so much you can't tolerate it another minute. The middle drawer of your desk, where you couldn't find a paper clip or a notepad in a hurry if your life depended on it, or your clothes closet, where you just spent an hour looking for your blue shirt. Or that thing that just gave you a sore shin or a scraped elbow—*never again!* Stuff you're tired of taking flak for might also be a good choice here, or anything that makes an all-too-public mess.

Private and personal things. You know those little stashes—clutter in boxes, containers, drawers, wallets, purses, and briefcases. Tackle boxes, toolboxes, jewelry boxes, old gifts, souvenirs, clippings, notes, grooming gewgaws you've grown out of—all that obsolete personal paraphernalia you've been fumbling through for years to get to the good stuff.

It often helps to start with little places and build up your courage for the big. If we start looking at our stuff as truckloads (which in some cases it is), we'll be pretty overwhelmed and reluctant to begin—no matter how clear this weekend's schedule might be. If you size it up as "loads" instead (cupboardsful instead of cellarfuls), you won't even flinch before starting. Every home has lots of little places to dejunk, such as the sock or the silverware drawer, the spice rack or the tie rack, the medicine chest or the cedar chest.

> Make yourself a "don't need" list: If you want a real revelation and learning experience next weekend, and a good nudge to get started, sit down or, better still, walk around and make a list of the things you have that you really don't need or use now. Little things and big things too (like houses, cars, boats, trailers, and campers).

This decluttering of little places will be easy, fast, and rewarding. And once you start using all the new extra room this gives you, you'll be really turned on to tackle the tonnage now. This is great bait for coaxing you into the wonderful world of decluttering. In fact, lay this book down and get going on some of this now!

The more decluttering you do, the faster and better you'll get at it, the more confidence you'll gain, and the more anti-clutter corpuscles you'll build up in your bloodstream. You'll begin to actually look forward to taking on your next project and to exercising your evermore refined skills on the next target area. You'll know you can do it and you'll be excited by how good you'll feel afterward.

Create Some Room to Work

When you're faced with wall-to-wall, floor-to-ceiling clutter such as in a junk room, storage bin, or attic, the first thing you want to do is make yourself some room to work. So start dejunking with the biggest things and the things within reach right now that are the easiest to eliminate.

Once you have a clearing, it helps to have an empty table in it for your smaller tools and supplies, and to use for sorting. If you can't find a table in the stash, a card table or folding table will do fine.

You will also need some room for sorting, and for those piles or boxes of stuff you collect as you sort, such as "Baby Things to Give Away" or "Books for the Used Book Store." It's always more efficient to collect a bunch or boxful of whatever before you start packing it up or carrying it off to its new home.

Dejunking doesn't necessarily mean trash it all. Almost everything benefits from condensing. Condensing is dejunking too—there often is some good amidst all that chaff. Mail or old papers, for example, are usually about three-quarters obsolete or unwanted stuff and packaging and one-quarter or less worthwhile things.

After you have room to maneuver, you can either tackle the stacks systematically from one end to the other or pick off the next pile that appeals to you, wherever it may be. Since the will to weed through something is more than half the battle, go with impulse whenever you can.

A collection of small things, such as a drawer full of odds and ends or a box of ancient who-knows-what, is often best emptied onto your tabletop or a drop cloth or old sheet on the floor. There's something about seeing stuff all spread out that revs up the "judging" cells in the brain, plus you have to pick things up to put them back in the box, so you'll be more prone to let them go.

If you are not the only inhabitant of your house, and you're working somewhere in the public domain—such as a linen closet in a hallway—beware of gutting the whole thing at once unless you've got the entire day to work on it. We pack-rats can really pack it in, and you will simply not believe how much can come out of there. It'll be frustrating to everyone if your time runs out while there are still piles and heaps out and around everywhere. Better to proceed one shelf or layer at a time in such situations, and to stick with one such project before starting a new one.

Persist with Your List

Once you get started, don't let yourself be interrupted or side-tracked. If you come across the long-lost pocketknife or watch in your excavations, or a truly amazing photo of yourself as a trim young thing, don't stop now to wow. Set that little treasure in the "treasure box" underneath your table, and keep on going. The same goes for sudden impulses to try and find the matching candlestick now that you've unearthed this one, or to sprint out to the shed and see if the rain fly to this lovely tent might still be around somewhere. Don't start making calls to see if you can still get parts for that old pressure cooker, either. If your friend Susie stops by to catch up on things, make a date for some other time or ask her if she minds keeping you company while you keep at it. Or talk her into taking away some stuff—use interruptions positively. Stick with dejunking till you've finished your target area or your quota of trashing time for the day.

As you work your way through your "too much," you may eventually start muttering to yourself and wondering why you kept this and that (and for so long). You might get a little disgusted or discouraged now as you realize what is at hand and ahead. You're often working in hot, cramped, and dusty places, and you don't have much support from others. You've done a lot, but there seems to be so much more to do. And worst of all is the emotional drain of going through all that old stuff, especially paper clutter or sentimental savings. But in any kind of clutter, really, there are all kinds of evidence of unachieved ambitions, past illusions, forgotten plans, failed good intentions, neglect, carelessness—even unkindness on our part. Three or four hours of plowing through things like this can leave us more exhausted than a day of ditch digging. So don't be surprised and don't be derailed by this. Expect it and carry on with your carrying out.

It may also help to:

Vary your dejunking diet. If you've done six hours of paper and you can't take any more, spend the last two hours on garden or garage junk. Alternating the types of projects you take on: indoor/outdoor, mostly mental/mostly physical, will help keep dejunker's dejection to a minimum.

Stop now and start again tomorrow. We almost always feel better the next morning about things. This is also a good reason to schedule the toughest dejunking assignments for early in the day, when you're still feeling fresh and optimistic. It's easy to say, "Well, I'll do an hour of that each night after I get home from work," but it's a lot harder to actually do.

Remind yourself of the rewards—how nice it will be to have an uncramped clothes closet at last, or how much more you'll enjoy this space when it's your new exercise room or a study rather than a junk room.

Some folks keep themselves going by forcing the issue. They start dejunking the yard now and invite everyone they know to a big lawn party at the end of the month or at the end of the summer.

Check out one of my other books on dejunking (see page ii), especially *Clutter's Last Stand, 2nd Edition*, to strengthen your sense of *why* you're doing all this. An hour or two of perusing these pages will get you going again, I guarantee it, and it'll be fun, too.

Is It Trash or Treasure? (How to Sift, Sort, and Select)

"Junk judging" is the very heart of decluttering—deciding what to keep and what should go. You probably had a good reason (at the time) to get each and every piece of your clutter. And you might think you need to keep each and every bit of it. But remember the stifling effect of too much, and that important principle called "thinning."

At first it seems to go against all good sense and decency, the idea of getting rid of perfectly good "whatever's." My first lesson in this came in the sugar beet fields of the record-crop-per-acre Magic Valley in Idaho. The beets were planted in spring, and before long the seedlings literally sprang out of the fertile ground. Then we went into the fields and hacked, cut, and hoed about three-quarters of those healthy little plants down, leaving only one plant every eight or ten inches, where before there were five or six. We did this with the carrots and the corn, too, seemingly a temporary insanity of destroying what was flourishing. But time proved it a wise and profitable move: With the room to grow, those little seedlings grew into large, beautiful plants, yielding a-plenty. Any that didn't happen to be thinned, left in initially healthy clumps, soon crowded each other and a dwarfed, scrawny clump of nothing was the result. And here is the kicker: If you waited too long to thin, it was too late. The plants were too massed and jammed together to be separated without harm. They were out of control and you could only sit back and watch the waste.

Likewise, people or places that are crowded by clutter in time become limited, distorted, and twisted. Here, too, thinning and pruning aids blooming. And when it comes to our stuff, now is the time.

Junk Judging Guidelines

How can you decide, as you stand before that pile of "too much," what is junk and what isn't?

First—Your Clutter Is Your Call

I receive requests constantly to make professional visits or house calls to deal with people's clutter for them. I've refused all such offers, at any price. There is just no way anyone else can judge the weight or worth of your treasures. Value has a great deal to do with inner emotion, and never can we know someone else's soul well enough to make a wise judgment call on their things.

You have to decide—your stuff is your business, not mine, your spouse's or family's, or a consultant's. Only you know your mind and heart, your dreams and values, and the point you've reached now. Only you know the history of your things and the strength of your ties to them. Do they fit you now, or not? *You* judge junk!

A teddy bear with both ears missing, serious stains, and leaking stuffing isn't junk if the kids use it and love it. A new Lexus car (that you don't drive often or really need) in your garage could be total junk. The *time* you've had something, or how much it *cost* isn't really a factor in the disposal decision, either. Who had it before or where you got it isn't really important either.

Try this little "judging" guideline sheet. For each piece of junk, think about the question, and then circle yes or no. (Honest answers, now!)

Junk Judging Guidelines

Value Factor	Question	Answer
Life enhancement	Will it enhance the quality of your life now or in the future?	Yes or No
Use/activity	It's there—do you really use it?	Yes or No
Fit	Does it, will it, fit anymore? (Or have you outgrown it?)	Yes or No
Place	Do you really have a place or space (on, in, or around you) for it?	Yes or No
Does it love YOU?	Does owning it bless, inspire, and expand you—does it love you back?	Yes or No

The Key Question to Ask Yourself

When sorting and deciding what goes and what stays, remember this: How long you've had something; how much it cost; who gave it to you, when, and why; whether it was hand-made or imported and all of that are not the determining factors for keeping something. Just quit loving things that have stopped loving you back. We outgrow many things—this is often a good thing—and we need to face the present and future without lugging along the past. So ask yourself the ultimate question with each article: "Does this now—or will it in the future—enhance my life (or the lives of others)?"

If the answer is no, a good, solid, clear-cut no, then get it out of your life any way you can. There is no room for "moderation" here—if something is worthless to you, there's no need to keep it around you!

~~~~~~

"An important word here is passion. If you are passionate about something, it is important to you and therefore not junk. If a thing or activity does not create passion or excitement or they have waned, then it's time to dejunk."

~~~~~~

Yes, You Can Get Rid of Things You Are Tired Of!

Dear Don,

When our six-year-old to-be-adopted daughter arrived by airplane from Texas, she had with her one suitcase of clothes, one suitcase of books, and three bushels of stuffed toys! Several months later I got after her about cleaning up her room, and she sat down on the floor, burst into tears, and screamed, "I have too much stuff!"

"Then get rid of some of it," I said.

She looked up, her face suddenly radiant, and said, "You mean I can?"

Two days later, we took two bushels of stuffed toys to the charity collection center. From the remaining bushel, she stored a few at her oldest sister's apartment for overnight stays, gave several away to neighbor children, and kept a modest few for herself. Now, at sixteen, she has exactly one teddy bear left from those three bushels. Meanwhile, her twin cousins, with whom she lived until she came to us, have filled a ten-foot-long built-in bookcase entirely with stuffed animals. And Alicia, every three or four months, carefully sorts her possessions and loads things she no longer uses into plastic bags for us to take *to the thrift store. Her built-in bookcase has one shelf of her favorite books, one shelf of photographs she likes to display, and one shelf strewn with flowers she dried herself with a few treasures such as a collection of seashells artistically arranged among them.*

But I don't think I will ever forget her awed delight at realizing she was actually allowed to get rid of things she was tired of. Sometimes she goes overboard—she has given away three beds, two dressers, a computer and printer, and a few chairs, but she will never be a slave to her possessions.

If In Doubt Throw It Out?

I really don't like the old adage, "If in doubt, throw it out." A lot of mistakes are made that way. I would counsel you to not be in doubt. *If in doubt, find out.* And *then* decide whether to keep it or throw it out.

I also disagree with the old saw, "If you haven't used it in six months (or a year), get rid of it." I haven't used my Scout uniform for several years, but I'm not going to get rid of it; haven't used my sleds for three years (not enough snow in Idaho the last three winters), but I'm not going to get rid of them. And I haven't used my fire extinguisher for fifteen years, and I'm surely not going to toss it out.

The length of time you've owned something is immaterial—two minutes could be too long and twenty years not long enough to own something. Asking yourself "Does this enhance my life?" or "Will it?" is the key—decide on the basis of use or honest potential use.

Remember: The Past Is to Learn From, Not Live In

We are slow to let go of what we used to be and that is good in a way. But the past is to learn from, not live in, and getting rid of what we used to be is, for the most part, a real plus. The old and the used-to-be are ballast that holds us back from our voyage to where we want to be, more than we ever imagine. If much of what you used to be wasn't really a blessing, it wasn't what you had in mind, or you never felt good about it, then dump it for sure. Get it out of the album, out of the records, out of the clothes closet, out of the attic— and leave some room for what you want to be.

Don't Backslide!

Backsliding (sneaking back to the garbage bag or Dumpster to recover something you've already ditched) can be a real problem for a packrat.

What we need, folks, is a computer mouse attached to our stuff, so we can move that little arrow to an item, then move the item over to a little garbage can icon, hit the button, and the thing is trashed, gone forever, unrecoverable. And if I were an inventor, this is what I would come up with, for the greatest of all clutter cures.

The very name "odds and ends" ought to give us a clue when it comes to making a judgment on value.

You need to dump something the day you determine it is detrimental to your daily living. Don't let it lie in "wake" in the parlor to be pawed over by others, who might think they need to review whether or not you should have cast it out. Resurrected clutter is a ghost you don't need around to haunt you any longer.

What about Those Antiques?

Like many of you, I have a soft spot for keepsakes and antiques, and an avid appreciation for them. I have a now world-famous cleaning museum, and I'm constantly on the lookout for new (old!) pieces for it. Antiques are well worth *ooh*ing and *ahh*ing over—they carry feelings, reminders, and lessons from the past that we all need for inner nourishment and a better future life. But too many fine antiques are either accidentally destroyed or buried in clutter, and thus are never available to be seen or used. Antiques lost in attics or piles are worthless to both the owner and the public. For many years now my mission has been to find such things, protect them, and make them productive. Why let them rust and ruin until they merit tossing?

Old Doesn't Always Mean "Gold"

One problem here is the tendency to think everything old is valuable, because that is far from the truth. We've all heard stories or watched a television show where an antique lamp or etching turns out to be worth $265,000! This may happen, but those are rare one-in-a-million chances, so don't let something you don't like or even have room for take up space forever because you hope it might be a treasure. In more than fifty years in the profession of helping people clean up and look after their possessions, and at least two decades of researching and writing about saved stuff, I have yet to see in person one single, bona fide trash-to-treasure story. At each of the stops on a major radio and TV tour I was on once, we asked callers and audiences to let us in on any incident wherein a great fortune was made from a piece of old saved stuff. Guess what? In all of those broadcasts, we received not one single response! That big "might" we often have in the back of our mind somewhere when it comes to old stuff often turns out to be a "mite" when it comes to value.

We all think our old stuff is going to be valuable someday, simply because it's old. But a goodly percent of old stuff is worthless.

So let's be more realistic about the stuff we keep, and weigh the cost of keeping something against its true chance of being valuable someday to your nearest and dearest or an outside market. Remember, 290 million other people in this country alone have garages, attics, basements, and storage sheds full of the same or similar stuff.

Make This Weekend the Moment of Truth!

If in doubt, find out now, instead of pushing the item in question to the back for later. If you run into something you feel has historic or collector value, deal with it this weekend, not later! Consult an expert and have it examined and appraised. When it comes to antiques, there are experts in everything from brass blowtorches to buttons, corkscrews to ship logbooks, old telephones to Boy Scout stuff, boxing to big band memorabilia, Civil War collectibles to cigar labels, oyster-related objects to old bottles.

One great discovery I've made visiting antique shops looking for old cleaning pieces for my museum is how competent the owners of such shops are, even in the smallest towns. These people have clubs and connections and an impressive expertise. They know where and how to get information for you if they don't have it. And best of all, I really trust these people. If you have a rare something worth $2,500, they aren't likely to tell you $25 or $250, and try to buy it. Their eyes will light up and they will be enthusiastic for you!

So walk in and ask or show—don't delay. Waiting has caused more waste of good stuff than all the floods and fires of the centuries.

If it is an antique, then act on it—take care of it, put it to work for others to see and benefit from. If you need money, sell it and invest the money in some better way.

No-Mess Access

What we do with the stuff we don't do away with is as important as the decision to keep it. If it ends up inaccessible again, we might just as well have ditched it. This is a good thing to keep in mind when making decisions. Keepers aren't really keepers if you have no place to put them for easy access. It's your call as to how and where to store them, but figure it out or *boot it out*!

Once you have your worthwhile things where you can get to them easily, don't wait forever to go through them again.

Let me give an example from my own life. At home, in the media, and as I have traveled around the country and the world, I have met so many sharp, insightful, incredibly helpful women that I started a drawer in my file cabinet called "The World's 100 Most Wanted Women." I anticipated perhaps hiring some of them or using them as consultants or research sources. I added to it over time and it finally got so full that there wasn't one single person I was following up on or sending copies of my new books to as I'd planned, because it wasn't a list of people—it was a mass of stuff. When something that would have been of interest to one of them did come up, or a time or place cropped up for meeting with one of them, I couldn't get to what I needed easily enough to benefit either of us.

Then I learned an important rule of storage: Don't just go through stored things, but go through them *often*. Our purposes, our intentions, and our reasons change daily, weekly, yearly—even hourly—and times and opportunities pass. Often, both the rhyme and the reason for which you originally kept something have totally faded and the matter is closed, so why keep it around and in the way of things?

Waiting years to go through things is too long. Going through your saved stuff every few months and freshening it up is pure pleasure. In a single hour one day, I reduced the "100 Most Wanted" drawer by two-thirds, and renewed some of the most beneficial contacts. The value in keeping anything is in keeping it current and instantly accessible.

Beware of "Junk Bunkers"

In your efforts to evict the excess in your life, beware of the two-edged sword called "organizers"—shelves, baskets, binders, boxes, racks, pigeonhole devices, containers of all kinds, even furnishings like china and curio cabinets. There is no end to the miracle devices today that, once bought, will "instantly put everything you have in order." Don't you believe it. First of all, you have to do the organizing, and second, organizers often just give us the excuses and means to keep and store more. Remember the first principle of packrattery: Stuff will accumulate proportionate to the space and place made available for it.

> Moving around or organizing things we ought to get rid of ends up just being a long-term game of musical chests (or drawers).

Clever organizers, just like a trash compactor in the home or office, can take a mass of clutter and condense it to a smaller size. The fact that it now takes up less space is so admirable that we forget it is still there—just as heavy, and just as useless. What needs to be removed from our place ought to be evicted now, not squeezed into a smaller, more convenient size to be carried around till later. Renaming things, or creating some elaborate filing system or category for them, doesn't change what they are. Clutter is still clutter even if it is housed in neat plastic containers.

Promises like "unique storage solutions" usually translate to, "We can stack it—clutter and all—higher, tighter, and neater." And for what closet organizing companies and the like can't fit in the closet, they will provide accessories for, to screw onto doors and walls and accommodate the rest. No matter how creatively arranged or superbly stacked, clutter is still clutter.

Flinch first when you see an organizer, then visualize what will end up in it, and you'll probably pass it by—and be glad you did.

> "My biggest mistake in dejunking was trying to organize what I needed to get rid of."

Don't get carried away with organizing stuff . . . carry away as much of it as you can first! You don't have to organize it if you don't have it. Most of us don't get rid of clutter, we just get a bigger box (or the biggest junk bunker of all—a bigger house!).

What Can You Do with What You Weed Out?

One good place to dispose of your clutter is via America's first answer for "too much" . . . the garage sale! Holding a garage sale will get things back into circulation, which is one solution. A garage sale also causes enough work, frustration, embarrassment, and reflection to inspire us next time to buy and keep less. God bless garage sales (as long as my wife doesn't go)!

Guidelines for Garage Sales (to really move that merchandise out)

Clean it—Use disinfectant cleaner and inform people "I've cleaned this with Slapacide." People fear other people's germs.

Price it—Not what you overpaid, or the "recovery" or "revenge" price, but more along the lines of, "Someone will haul this off for me and it will have a good home."

Display it—Anything up off the ground or sidewalk sells better, so make or rent tables and cover them.

Pool it—Combo presentations (yours and your neighbors' goods) draw more of each other's relatives, and will double or triple sales.

Another good way to dispose of your "weed-outs" comes from a relieved packrat in Madison, Wisconsin:

"One thing that has helped me to get rid of stuff to which I feel emotionally attached is to give it to individuals rather than institutions. I had a large number of books about the Middle Ages, for example— many of them beautifully illustrated. I knew I'd never read them again, but somehow I couldn't bear to part with them. Then I met a young man who was majoring in German medieval history in college. His delight and gratitude in receiving the books somehow filled the emotional hole created by my giving them up. Similarly, I recently packed up loads of quality clothes in excellent condition. Instead of donating them to a Goodwill store, I brought them to a local shelter for men recovering from addictions. Seeing some of the men face-to-face who would be wearing my clothes gave me a feeling of warmth that more than compensated for any sense of loss over the clothing I was surrendering."

Don't let creeping doubts override the impulse to be generous. There are plenty of people and places out there that can benefit from your culls!

Chapter 6
Clutter at a Glance

This chapter is a short course in the most common and troublesome kinds of clutter inhabiting the modern home and office—where they live, what they look like, what harm they do us, and how to make short work of them!

CAVE CLUTTER

(Clutter that is out of sight but out of control!)

- **Under the bed**
- **In the closet**
  (the number-one cave)
- **In drawers**
- **In cabinets**
- **In cupboards**
- **In bookcases**
- **In refrigerators**
- **In freezers**
- **In junk rooms**
- **In storage units**
- **In basements**
- **In attics**
- **In sheds**

SUMMARY:

Our lives' leftovers languish in caves such as the examples just given. Much of this stuff (except for seasonal clothes and holiday decorations) is where it is because it doesn't get much use. It is lying in wake, awaiting a burial of some kind, though other clutter has temporarily buried much of it. You might say it's in the coffin, but not yet in the ground!

The amount of cave clutter we have usually parallels our decision-stalling ability, and because all this stuff is hidden, we think it doesn't hurt. Cave clutter loves to laugh at us as we move it in from somewhere else, cram it in, shuffle it from shelf to shelf, pore over it, hunt through it, fold and refold it, arrange and rearrange it, forever trying to fit more in while we dream up excuses for it. Often as much as 60 percent or more of cave clutter is unneeded and, if we are honest about it, unwanted.

SOLUTION:

To clean out a cave, you have to go in, not just keep passing by. That means you dig all the way in, or else what is in back of, under, and behind will remain there forever. Up to now we have just removed the overflow or in-the-way stuff, dodging anything that is difficult to get through or around. Pull it all out, and you'll know what to eliminate.

As for the good stuff, condense it and box it (don't leave it rattling around loose),  and mark the box on all four sides and the top with a permanent marker. This will jog your memory or help others the next time around. Otherwise, you or others will be forced to open and go through every box, when you're getting ready to move, desperate to find something, or faced with a fire or flood situation. Or, when someone else (after your departure from this planet) has to deal with it all.

When you're finished, you'll have eliminated the fire, odor, or safety hazard; regained the use of some of your most convenient storage space; and made room for fresh and important future stuff.

GOAL:

Being able to open the door to any of these areas without embarrassment, and find what you need without a headlamp! And no more overcrowding.

For more on cave clutter see Chapter 5 of *Clutter's Last Stand*, Chapters 6 and 8 of *For Packrats Only*, and Chapter 6 of *Clutter Free! Finally & Forever*.

ON TOP OF STUFF

- Keys
- Change and coins
- Prescription pills and medications
- Clothing
- Gloves
- Wallets
- Cufflinks
- Jewelry
- Books
- Watches
- Pens
- Cards
- Instructions to things
- Directions to places
- Junk mail
- Bills
- Catalogs
- Newspapers
- Magazines
- Hankies
- Cosmetics
- Grooming aids
- Tools
- Finished or unfinished projects
- Things on their way somewhere

SUMMARY:

The accessible "tops" in our living space were meant for purposes other than storing and stacking. Covering them with clutter causes confusion, breakage, and lack of privacy, and impedes use and cleaning of the item this happens to be the top of. When you consider those cluttered tops of dressers, chests of drawers, counters, tables, refrigerators, workbenches, night tables, end tables, desks, window ledges, bookcases, and credenzas, it all adds up to a top traffic jam.

SOLUTION:

Putting things on a top overnight, or while you're actually using the area, is great—you have a place to put something and you put it there. The problem here is not in using the top, but in leaving the mess behind when you're done. When you clear your project out, clear it *all* out. It only takes seconds to transfer things to a drawer, cupboard, box, shelf, or compartment somewhere near the top area, so you can keep a clean, clear top. Hanging tools and other things right over the place where they will be used is even handier than heaping them on top!

GOAL:

Tops that are clear look good, are easy to clean, and can be *used* for whatever they need to be used for.

For more on trimming down "top of" clutter, see Chapter 8 of *For Packrats Only,* and Chapters 9 and 10 of *The Office Clutter Cure.*

One woman sent me a long list of everything unneeded she found on her dresser tops, from broken flutes to Harley-Davidson patches, old eyeglasses to miniature chess sets to used Q-tips. Her final comment was, "It is truly amazing what can fit on the 12" x 36" top of a dresser."

CLOTHES CLUTTER

- Suits
- Dresses
- Blouses
- Shirts
- Skirts
- Slacks
- Sweaters
- Jackets
- Robes
- Coats
- Formal wear
- Athletic wear
- Sweatshirts
- T-shirts
- Uniforms
- Vests
- Coveralls
- Shorts
- Swimsuits
- Long johns
- Novelty clothes
- Shoes
- Socks
- Scarves
- Gloves
- Ties and belts
- Hats
- Caps

SUMMARY:

Wardrobes are often one of our worst cases of "too much." We must be reminded, it seems, that we have only one head, two hands, two feet, and a torso. You can waste a lot of life pawing through closets and drawers full of clothes, worrying about fashion, matching, moths, and storage of rarely or never used apparel. Just because you paid for it once doesn't mean you have to keep on paying. If you had just one of each of the clothes listed above, you would have about thirty pieces to wear, wash, and worry about. If you have two of each, that means sixty, and three of each, ninety. Need I go on? Too much!

SOLUTION:

The judgments here will be easy if you remember that the bottom line on clothes is wearing, not wishing. Clothing clutter is mostly vanity motivated, so your clothes quotient right now should tell you something about your personality.

Six Smart Ways to Clear the Closet

- Outfits that don't fit are out!
- Anything uncomfortable should go!
- Retire what looks better on the hanger than on you.
- Too nice to stain may be too nice to remain.
- Panic- or impulse-purchased clothes are almost always pass-on-able.
- Herds of rarely worn hats and shoes require year-round roundup.

GOAL:

An uncrowded closet that gives you easy, wrinkle-free selection and cuts out all that rummaging and try-on and fretting time.

For more on coping with clothes clutter, see Chapter 8 of *Clutter's Last Stand,* Chapter 8 of *For Packrats Only,* and Chapter 6 of *Clutter Free! Finally & Forever.*

FURNITURE CLUTTER

- Overstuffed chairs
- Wing-backed chairs
- Old kitchen chairs
- Captain's chairs
- Beanbag chairs
- Blow-up chairs
- Extra office chairs
- Recliners
- Couches
- Sofas
- Love seats
- Futons
- Hide-a-beds
- Roll-away beds
- Desks
- Shelves
- Beds
- Dressers
- Nightstands
- Armoires
- Cribs
- Lamps
- Coffee tables
- Dining room tables
- End tables
- Card tables
- TV trays
- Table leaves
- Hutches

- Knickknack and whatnot and showcase and corner cupboards
- Baker's racks
- Buffets
- Butler carts
- Ottomans
- Stools
- Cushions

SUMMARY:

Most of us have 25 percent more furniture than we need or are currently using, and sad to say, we are always looking and shopping for more to replace some that may not really need replacing. Most furniture doesn't wear out (some actually lasts centuries, not just lifetimes). Furniture can ugly out from poor care or lack of repair, or we can just get tired of it. But we have a hard time letting furniture of any kind go, so instead we put it in the basement or another room, or store it in the garage or at Grandma's house. We fight unneeded furniture, hoard it, and refuse to give it away until mice, sun, rain, or people running into it finally do it in. Then we can throw it out.

SOLUTION:

1. Be very slow to replace furniture. Once you start thinking about and looking at new furniture, there is no stopping and you can do real dumb things.

2. Remember how when you first moved away from home or got married, how long and well you got along with "Early Packing Crate" furnishings?

3. Once you commit to the new, you need to provide for the old at the same time. Don't move one thing in without a clear and committed destination for the piece being replaced. Old furniture motto: "Out of the room, out of your life."

4. If you need furniture only for a while, rent it, borrow it, or use the floor. Nothing is worse than having lots of furniture to move and a too-small house to put it in.

5. Buy the best when you buy the first time and most of your furniture clutter problems will be over. You'll be so poor you can't buy any more and the quality of

the pieces you do have will eliminate the need to buy any more.

GOAL:

Have only the furniture you need and like, and have it where it belongs, for a long, long time. Keep it clean and in good repair so that people will treat it as they should.

For more on freeing yourself of unnecessary furniture, see Chapter 6 of *For Packrats Only*, pages 54, 61, and 62; see Chapter 3 of *The Office Clutter Cure*; and pages 137–140 of *Clutter Free! Finally & Forever.*

* Administrative Professional or Boss's Day gifts
* Valentine's Day gifts
* At least twenty other gift-giving days
* Housewarming gifts
* Friendship gifts
* Going-away gifts
* Coming home gifts
* Wedding gifts
* Retirement gifts
* Promotion gifts
* Graduation gifts
* Anniversary gifts
* Plaques
* Trophies
* Awards
* Pins
* Badges

GIFTS

* Christmas gifts
* Hanukkah gifts
* Birthday gifts
* Mother's Day gifts
* Father's Day gifts
* Grandparent's Day gifts

SUMMARY:

Sure, they aren't of our own choosing, but we're the ones who keep them—for what, and for how long? "But someone gave it to me" is not a valid excuse for entombing something forever. Black eyes and rattlesnakes can be given, too. Gifts are meant to convey the best of feelings, not to become a burden.

SOLUTION:

Believe and practice "It's the thought that counts."

Remember, a gift is just the transmitter of affection—not the affection itself. When you get a gift, concentrate on the giver ("How thoughtful so-and-so is!") rather than on the object he or she happened to give. Savor the love, care, kindness, cash, and maybe even hard work that went into the gift, and how genuinely the giver intended to please you. And then deal with it like any other item in your dejunking program—do I like this, do I need it, or not? If you don't ever intend to use it, don't really want to look at it, and refuse to display it, better to move it out.

If there are any regrettables among those receivables:

- Use them, put them in service, wear them out.
- Trade or exchange them for something you do want.
- Take a photo of them for sentiment and then pass them on.
- Give them to any admirer of them.
- Leave them lying around in public in a nice box.
- Dissect them for usable parts.
- Give or will them back to the givers.

GOAL:

As much as you can, free yourself of the politics of overdone gift giving and receiving, and reciprocating and acknowledging (and then tending). Don't be a junk gift giver yourself. Visit people when they are sick or in need instead. It's the best gift of all, the most remembered, and creates zero clutter. Caring for the sick and lonely can seldom reach "too much."

For more on graceful gift divestment, see Chapter 6 of *Clutter's Last Stand* and Chapter 8 of *For Packrats Only*.

PHOTOS

- Slides
- Color prints
- Black and whites
- Polaroids
- Videos
- Memory cards
- Computer images
- Film—used and unused
- Negatives
- Portraits
- Snapshots
- Kids' school pictures
- Pictures of graduations, sweethearts, weddings, and trips

SUMMARY:

Photographs have one purpose and value—to be seen! Basements and attics across the country house photos of every type, all waiting for . . . what? For the cellar to flood or attic to overheat, so we can weep and groan over our lost heritage. Photos today are easy to take, and can easily multiply to too many to keep track of. The valuable ones are lost in the piles or on computer files and are never seen or appreciated. Why do we keep every single thing that ever comes back from the developer? Those fuzzy pictures aren't going to come into focus, nor the red-eyed ones fade, nor those missing heads grow back on. While we're at it, how many cameras (and accessories) do you have? How many of them actually work? How many do you *use*?

SOLUTION:

The solution is a simple "S.O.S.":

S: Sort

Go through all your photos. Toss or delete the ruined, fourth-rate, and unidentifiable ones. Trim the total number down, organize them by subject, year, or whatever makes sense to you, and then identify the ones that really matter. Doing this with another person or persons is a good way to speed the process. Sort the pictures into separate piles to be copied, enlarged, or framed. Toss those envelopes that pictures come back in from the developer—they only add to the pile. Negatives are small and thin; a lifetime's worth can be stored in a little light-tight box. Trash obviously worthless photos, put the others into labeled envelopes, and keep them forever.

As for digital pictures, there are many Web sites that you can upload your photos to, and they will develop your prints and send them back by mail. This is one way to weed out and develop only the ones you love. Digital files can be stored on a computer hard drive or archived onto a disk. Be aware, however, that disks can get ruined and computers can crash, taking all your beloved photo images with them. A storage alternative for your digital photos would be storing them in cyberspace on a Web site such as *www.gmail.com* or the like. Photo memory cards that fit in your camera are another way to store digital photos and there are special cases to keep them in.

O: Offer

Select and send off the photos that don't mean much to you, but will touch or enhance others' lives. Include the negative if you can find it or a jpeg or the like, along with a note, and it might result in getting a valuable picture back from them.

S: Show

Photos always have a place, at home or at work, on walls, in stands, in albums or scrapbooks. Mount the best photos and put them up on the wall or somewhere else where they are accessible, organized, and can be seen. Or convert them to video. Enlarge good shots and send them as gifts.

Once photos are out of boxes and into full view or appreciative ownership, beholders and new owners will weep in your arms for joy at the memory stimuli. Photos can teach, motivate, inspire, and create interest and valuable relationships.

GOAL:

All the photos you have, and any being taken now or in the future, made instantly accessible and usable. Using photos to actively enhance life, not just record it.

For more on putting photos in focus, see Chapter 7 of *Clutter's Last Stand* and pages 69–70 of *For Packrats Only*.

MAGAZINES

* Professional magazines
* Technical magazines
* Household magazines
* Entertainment magazines
* In-flight magazines
* Women's magazines
* Men's magazines
* Children's magazines
* News magazines
* Religious magazines

* Association and organization magazines
* Food magazines
* Gardening magazines
* Woodworking magazines
* Automobile magazines

This list could go on to fill a book!

SUMMARY:

First there were twenty, then the number jumped to 200. Today, there are thousands of different magazines, so if you think you can manage to keep up, forget it! Magazines, especially the large-circulation ones, aren't usually a prime source of information; you won't usually find much in one that takes a solid stand (truth is controversial, and too many advertisers would be offended). Magazines are getting more and more expensive ($3 or more an issue). And one "hooker" or lead article on the cover in bold letters is supposed to justify buying the whole thing. Magazines are hard to keep up with (twelve magazines a month is 1,200 pages to deal with—forty a day!), and guilt-producing when we don't.

They pile up fast in the living room and the attic.

SOLUTION:

The majority of most magazines is advertising, which is updated monthly, so keeping them doesn't really make sense. Magazines should be handled once—scan them as soon as you get them. Remove or copy the few things you want to read later or save, and chuck the rest in the recycle bin. Magazines take zero concentration, so if you keep them handy to deal with during waiting time, commercials, or at those early or late hours of the day, you can pick and peruse the edifying and discard the rest. If you get a backup of five magazines to read, you are beginning to be buried. Cutting down the number of subscriptions you have and keeping up with the reading are the solutions for magazine "too much."

GOAL:

Stopping subscriptions to magazines that you don't process promptly. Reading this month's before next month's arrives. Saving only

articles you really want—never the whole magazine.

For more on magazines, see Chapter 7 of Clutter's Last Stand and For Pack-rats Only, and Chapter 6 of Clutter Free! Finally and Forever.

BOOKS

- Cookbooks
- Novels
- How-to guides
- Reference books
- Idle reading
- Children's books
- Schoolbooks
- Professional books
- Directories
- Manuals
- Record books
- Tally books
- Religious books
- Racy books
- Gift books
- Encyclopedias

- Atlases
- Secondhand books
- Antiques
- Borrowed books
- Long-overdue library books

SUMMARY:

Books fill our shelves and the shelves of bookstores, and new ones are pouring forth from the presses at the rate of more than 60,000 a year. Add in what we have piled and stored, and what we've borrowed, loaned, or lusted after, and we have too much.

Because books were once rare and precious, we hesitate to relieve our shelves of them. But today, most books are produced quickly and inexpensively, and the fact that something is in book form is no guarantee of quality. Only about 20 percent of the books we keep around are actually used or even looked at occasionally, and a book has value only when and if it is read. Books are *heavy* and they take up a lot of room.

SOLUTION:

Books we could do without usually fall into the following categories:

Obsolete/outofdate—anything from old phone directories to *Factory Outlet Guide 1998*

Damaged—broken, dog-chewed, ripped, or water-stained

Unfinished—so dull we haven't made it beyond page 30 in three starts

Gift books—we didn't want it and won't read it, but it's brand new

Salvaged—saved from extinction, for what reason is still unclear

Book club book—by-default shelf-filler

Decorator—book kept to impress onlookers/intellectuals

Blinded by the binding—books with beautiful leather bindings and pages that will never be cracked

After sorting books, proceed to one of the following:

- Dump, sell, recycle.
- Reroute to someone who cares.

* Strip or rip out the few pages that were all you really wanted anyway.
* Read—dust it off, read it, and keep it for the whole family to enjoy.

Always determine "shelf life" yourself. Only you know your book needs, wants, and wishes. Once your library is culled, purged, and purified, you can savor what you have. This also saves dusting and forever criticizing yourself for never getting at those books.

GOAL:

Some breathing room in your mind and on your bookshelves. Easy access to your good and beloved books, and room for new, better books to come into your life.

For more on taking a hard look at books, see Chapter 7 of _Clutter's Last Stand_ and _For Packrats Only,_ and Chapter 6 of _Clutter Free! Finally and Forever._

"Apart from a few favorite cookbooks, well and often used, I save only individual recipes (and only those which have been tried and tested and found worthy of repeated use). These slip easily into plastic sleeves that I keep in a binder. I have an index at the front which I update every couple of years (a ten-minute task). I even (gasp!) slice the page I want right out of a cookbook to keep, and give away the book."

ENTERTAINMENT CLUTTER

Unwanted, broken, or obsolete:

- TVs
- VCRs
- CD and DVD players
- Sound systems
- Boom boxes
- Musical instruments
- Videotapes
- Video games
- Audio cassettes
- Records
- Earphones
- Antennas
- Speakers
- Programs
- Performance debris
- Cards
- Games
- Puzzles and other adult pacifiers
- Entertainment centers (the biggest junk bunkers of all)

SUMMARY:

The right to be entertained is one of the rights we, the modern generation, have added to the Constitution. Seems like the desire to be amused is gaining on the sex and hunger drives. We look for that entertainment from the outside instead of the inside, and so we have equipped our homes, cars, buildings, and body with devices to feed us sounds and sensations to get us through the day. The original "one radio for entertainment" has grown to take up an entire wall or room of the home, in which we have installed every entertainment device imaginable, almost letting media make our lives.

SOLUTION:

Cut down the volume of intake of all those "too much" entertainments. Use entertainment to refresh yourself, not to occupy all your free time. Balance what you have by way of entertainment equipment and what you need. If you don't use something, sell it or give it away.

Face up to the music or other fun stuff (CDs, DVDs, tapes, etc.) you ran to the register with but don't really dig. Dump any you aren't really proud to own, and sell or donate the rest.

If parts are no longer available for something, it would cost a small fortune to repair, or there's no way of getting rid of the static on it, do you really still want it? Try not to buy CDs you haven't heard, rent rather than buy movies you aren't going to watch again, and avoid joining music or video clubs.

GOAL:

Find entertainment within yourself, so you won't have to keep tuning in and out.

For more on tuning out entertainment clutter, see Chapter 6 of *Clutter's Last Stand* and page 75 of *For Packrats Only.*

CARRY-ALONG CLUTTER

- Contents of wallets, pockets, purses, cosmetic cases, briefcases
- Photos
- Puzzles
- Keys
- Keychains
- Checkbooks
- Address books
- Writing gear
- Planners
- Cards
- Tickets
- Coupons
- Coins
- Tokens
- Grooming tools
- Cosmetics
- Good-luck charms
- Nibbles
- Breath sweeteners
- Medications and pills
- Cameras
- Clothes
- Weather protection gear
- Personal protection gear

SUMMARY:

This clutter is strictly personal and is viewed as a vital operational tool—the resources we need to make it through the average day. But a good 40 percent of this carry-along clutter could be done without, and makes for a far bigger load to lug than we want or need. All of this weight makes us look and feel like a pack mule.

SOLUTION:

Spread all of your carry-around clutter out on the bed so you can weigh it mentally and physically. Seeing your clutter laid out this way will convince you that hauling stuff like this around has to be the silliest of all excess. Your goal, even if you keep all the categories of stuff you see here, is to reduce the weight by at least a third. Cut six credit cards down to two, get rid of all obsolete keys and leave the seldom-used ones home, dump any unnecessary medications, weed down that grooming gear, go to smaller versions of everything. Condense and miniaturize, and drop those pennies in the piggybank. Move to a smaller wallet or purse. Review everything (from wallet photos to lucky charms to insurance and library cards) for long-out-of-date stuff. This is one area of clutter only *you* can deal with, and you can and should show some guts. Purge those purses and pockets!

GOAL:

The goal is to travel light, unless you have a baby, in which case you are excused for up to thirty pounds of infant stuff—necessities and accessories. You want to be 100 percent up to date, and not have to feel or slap your pockets or rummage for even a second when you need or are asked for something.

For more on jettisoning carry-along clutter, see Chapter 8 of *Clutter's Last Stand,* Chapter 7 of *For Packrats Only,* and Chapters 3 and 4 of *The Office Clutter Cure.*

FITNESS CLUTTER

- Jogging shoes
- Running shoes
- Aerobic shoes
- Vitamin bottles
- Water bottles (and straws and belt loops and packs for same)
- Treadmills
- Pads and mats
- Benches and belts and tables
- Weights of all kinds
- Bags and totes of every shape and description
- T-shirts from every road race, walk, or competition
- Special bras and straps and jox and sox
- Knee braces
- Wrist supports and back supports
- Magic stretchers and squeezers
- Sweat suits
- Sweatbands
- Hip and tummy reducers
- Bust builders
- Punching bags
- Exer-cycles
- Video workouts from every major supermodel and star

SUMMARY:

This is one of the fastest-multiplying forms of modern-day clutter. We buy the latest and the greatest but hang on to every old club and racquet, too. Motivated by the latest studies on cholesterol or calorie consumption (or a look in the mirror), we go hog-wild getting tools, machines, gear, and gadgets of all kinds, along with books and videos, to get in shape. Most of these are soon stashed in the closet, under the bed, or in the basement. But we keep buying new ones. The other day I saw a fellow carrying a new exercise machine into his house, walking right past the hired guys mowing his lawn. The only real exercise that results from many of these machines is the extra walking you have to do to step around them, the effort involved in moving them from room to room (trying to find somewhere out of the way to keep them), cleaning around them, and the extra hours you have to work to pay for them. The only things in the house getting a workout are the floor and walls—from the weight of these antiweight machines.

SOLUTION:

1. Eat less. If you are buying fitness gizmos mainly to lose weight, lessening your food intake will probably give quicker results.
2. Buy used stuff so you can easily jettison it when it doesn't work or you get tired of it.
3. If you really want to get fit, this is a better investment: Have your doctor check you over and then join a class at a gym that is right for your age, condition, and the kind of fitness you aspire to. This is one case where together-ness can be a big help.
4. If you have no health restrictions, jog or walk rather than saunter. Use the streets and parks instead of your house to exercise, and there will be zero need for stuff.

(You can also buy a new shovel or rake and use it. Or get a second job lifting grain sacks.)

GOAL:

Keeping in shape without tons of fitness trappings and paraphernalia—such as walking instead of riding wherever we can and getting exercise by keeping our house and yard in shape.

For more on freeing yourself of fitness clutter, see Chapters 6 and 7 of *For Packrats Only.*

"I use my treadmill in the bedroom to hang my extra clothes on."

SPORTS CLUTTER

- Balls
- Bats
- Mitts
- Racquets
- Cleats
- Helmets
- Shoes
- Jerseys
- Hats, hats, hats
- More hats

- Special tinted glasses
- Socks
- Tackle boxes
- Maps
- Lures
- Nets
- Strings
- Float tubes and appendages
- Guns and knives
- Boots
- Tents
- Stoves
- Bandages
- Uniforms
- Packs
- Cameras
- Photos
- Trophies
- Gloves
- Shin guards
- Wrist and ankle braces
- Elbow and knee pads
- Mouthpieces
- Goggles
- Magazines
- Canteens
- Pads
- Vests
- Floats
- Boats
- Skis
- Poles
- Parkas

SUMMARY:

The more "sporty" we become, the more we multiply our trappings as "new and improved" and "recommended-by-the-professionals" things come along. But sports are often a brief phase of life, or just a passing fancy. We, or our children, are into something briefly, and then we are in it as spectators. (Meaning that all the gear that made us go, could probably go now.)

SOLUTION:

1. When you lose your enthusiasm for a sport, donate the leftover equipment to some kids somewhere. There is always a new and needy generation of fresh, eager youths to literally fill your shoes.

2. If something means a great deal to you still, even though you're not using it, mount it. If there is a jersey, ball, bat, fishing rod, or one or two other treasures in the sports pile that hold memories you just cannot let go of, good! Find a way to mount it on a plaque or in a frame. Then hang it up and savor it

while the crowd cheers again silently.

3. Much athletics or sports gear that's had its day is in the way. It might be used again (or more often) if it were contained and at least gotten out of our everyday way. Big plastic tubs are great for this.

GOAL:

The sports equipment you do use or want to keep make easily accessible. And what you and the kids have outgrown, pass on so that others may enjoy it as much as you did.

For more on clearing the field of sports clutter, see Chapter 7 of *For Packrats Only*, p. 114 of *Clutter Free!*, and Chapter 6 of *Clutter's Last Stand*.

PAPER CLUTTER

- Letters
- Junk mail
- Notes
- Reports
- Memos
- Ads
- Brochures
- Fliers
- Files
- Photocopies
- Clippings
- Receipts
- Catalogs
- Cards
- Envelopes
- Bills
- Magazines
- Newspapers
- Newsletters
- Warranties and instructions

SUMMARY:

We probably acquire at least 100 new pieces of paper per day, and that number is only increasing. All that paper piles up, and it turns us into diggers and hunters; it makes us late, takes up space, hurts our image, and confuses us. It breeds indecision and blocks relationships. And it doesn't self-destruct. Paper weight, once a nice little knickknack, is now a real problem.

SOLUTION:

1. The key is to condense the daily paper stream as soon as it comes in. Separate the piles into the fresh arrivals and the keepers.
2. Sort the backlog quickly into four categories:

Out—The awful, the obsolete, the un-understandable, the uninteresting, the unneeded. TOSS, HAVE IT TRANSLATED, OR RECYCLE IT!

Route—Paper that is out of place or belongs to others should go to a different department or be moved to storage. SEND IT TO WHEREVER IT BELONGS.

Doubt—Things to read, answer, process, and think over. TAKE WITH YOU TO DIGEST (and deal with them the moment you do!).

Sprout—Your good ideas, your dream projects, long-lost documents, leads, and addresses, etc. FILE SO YOU CAN FIND THEM, or scan them onto the computer.

GOAL:

More working space! Being ahead, not behind, and able to locate things instantly, with no apologizing anymore. Reclaiming 100 percent of that time lost rummaging and hunting.

For more on shearing through paper clutter, see Chapter 7 of *Clutter's Last Stand* and *For Packrats Only*, Chapter 6 of *Clutter Free! Finally & Forever*, and Chapters 5, 9, and 10 *The Office Clutter Cure*.

PACKAGING CLUTTER

- Boxes
- Wrappers
- Bags
- Plastic sacks
- Empty Cool Whip containers (the queen of container clutter)
- Jugs
- Bottles
- Cookie tins
- Bubble wrap

- "Ghost droppings" (Styrofoam peanuts)
- Crates
- Egg cartons
- Foil
- Pie tins
- Mailing enclosures of any kind
- Yes, even those lovely reinforced computer boxes

SUMMARY:

The original packaging served well once, and if it can do so again, great! But keeping every single item of packaging on your payroll "until you need it" is often a cost higher than the purchase of new enclosures. Packaging clutter is a prime fire, rodent, roach, and termite hazard, and who really has a place to keep packaging clutter? When we do need a container to ship or repackage something, our chances of finding something that fits in the midst of all this are almost nil. (Claiming these are "craft supplies" is no excuse.)

SOLUTION:

Selectivity is the key here. It makes both environmental and economic sense to have some containers around—for mailing, storing, or carrying things, or to send other junk away in. So:

1. First eliminate all the defective stuff—flimsy and sawed-off boxes; the water-damaged, crushed, mildewed, and chewed-up items; the holey sacks, rusty cans, dented tins, etc.

2. Pick out the primo containers and put them to work right now.

3. Then take about half the amount of containers you think you will need in the future and put them back in storage stacked inside each other. But this time locate them in such a way that they don't take up important central storage space, and so that you can find them when you need them. Just keep one or two cardboard boxes, stacked inside each other. Cardboard boxes can be stored much more efficiently if you break them down, but putting them back together is a pain.

4. Recycle or trash all the rest.

5. Getting in the fling of it as new boxes and bags flow in will help keep the packaging stream under control. You can also share the extras with friends and neighbors who are "looking for boxes for a move," and the like.

GOAL:

Not keeping any used packaging around that doesn't have an honest chance of being reused.

For more on packing out packaging clutter, see Chapter 8 of *For Packrats Only* and Chapter 6 of *Clutter Free! Finally & Forever.*

SENTIMENTAL STUFF

* Keepsakes
* Charms
* Corsages
* Souvenirs
* Diaries
* Ribbons
* Letters and notes

* Poems
* Awards and trophies
* Jewelry
* Antiques
* Locks of hair
* Dishes
* Cups
* Collections
* Homemade items
* Broken valuables
* Coins
* Programs
* Clippings
* Clothing
* Photos
* School papers
* Scrapbooks

This is a never-ending list!

SUMMARY:

Much of this IS valuable, because things like this can be the cornerstones of posterity, the markers of a trail (or trial) you don't want to forget. Keeping a token can keep a memory alive and preserve insights and feelings we'd all be lost without. But when you start feeling sorry for sentimental stuff, or keeping it begins to punish you instead of give you pleasure, it's time to point your compassion in a better direction.

SOLUTION:

Give your sentimental stuff the old one-two knockout:

1. Cull. Time takes a toll on sentimental stuff—we outlive and outgrow a lot of it. It served its time and is ready for pardon, so release it. If not only the item but the memories it held are faded and worn (or simply something you'd now like to forget), let it go. If you find this hard to do because you have lingering doubts about a particular piece of sentimental savings, you can photograph it or miniaturize it. Clip just one button off that old moth-eaten sweater, or a bit of the lace trim from that old camisole, before you drop it in the Dumpster or charity collection bin.

2. Activate. You kept these things for a reason—to show, share, and be inspired by them. So do it! Get some value out of those valuables. Find a way to make them active instead of passively storing them in a trunk or shed somewhere. Reposi-tion them, repaint them, or revive them. Convert them to something you can use in everyday life—mount them, frame them, hang them, move them to somewhere you can see and enjoy them, share them, maybe even flaunt them. They need to be in action, not in a hole somewhere. You might even want to label some of those that could be appreciated by others.

GOAL:

Weed it down to what really matters, and then make it part of your life!

For more on coming to terms with sentimental clutter, see Chapter 6 of *Clutter's Last Stand*, Chapter 8 of *For Packrats Only*, and Chapter 6 of *Clutter Free! Finally & Forever*.

THE "FIXABLES"

- Things that aren't working
- Broken things
- Things with parts missing
- Things that are obsolete
- Dull things
- Out-of-tune things
- Cracked things
- Frozen things
- Scorched things
- Rusted things
- Chipped things
- Stained things
- Rotted things
- Rodentized things
- "The old one" from anything we did fix

SUMMARY:

We've all got plenty of these . . . waiting for parts; time to fix it; a miraculous recovery; or a mate, neighbor, or talented in-law to come help us "heal" it. We feel guilt or sympathy for these things in their present condition; that is one reason we still have

them. We forget, all too easily, that if it doesn't work, it isn't working for us. Instead, we are working for it—storing it, explaining it, shuffling it from place to place. A big part of our excess pounds of objects, and our mental load, is on this "to be repaired" list.

SOLUTION:

Own not one thing that doesn't work or is wounded. Fix it now or find a different future for it. Complete this Repair Checklist for each of your fixables.

REPAIR CHECKLIST: Is it honestly fixable?

Will I use it again when it's fixed, and for what?
☐ **Yes** OR ☐ **No**

Are parts and refills really available for it?
☐ **Yes** OR ☐ **No**

Can I really fix this myself (do I have the talent and time)?
☐ **Yes** OR ☐ **No**

Is there a convenient/expert place to have it repaired?
☐ **Yes** OR ☐ **No**

Will the end result justify the cost of fixing: labor, parts, shipping, phone bills, driving time, the search to find someone who can fix it, having a second person work on it after the first one fails to fix it, etc.?

☐ Yes OR ☐ No

Do I have a reasonable place to keep it until it's fixed?

☐ Yes OR ☐ No

GOAL:

Get rid of it, or restore it.

For more on facing down "gonna fix it" clutter, see Chapter 4 of *Clutter's Last Stand*, Chapter 7 of *For Packrats Only*, and Chapters 3 and 4 of *The Office Clutter Cure*.

SOMEDAY STUFF

- Partly done projects
- Unopened kits
- Furniture to finish, restore, or haul off
- Old carpets we meant to put down somewhere
- Letters and books to finish
- Good intentions not acted upon
- Apologies unmade

- Trips or visits we wanted to make
- Aged chemicals, paint, and seeds
- Things to wear or to try someday
- Piles of things marked "To the Kids," "To Be Recycled," or "To the Dump"

. . . All sitting in the cellar, attic, junk room, or shed, waiting—and weighting—on *you*.

SUMMARY:

Someday stuff is the champion of the scale tilters—the real heavyweight. What is it? The kept but unfinished, the good intentions, the hopes and ambitions withered on the vine. Some of this might still deserve its day, but you need to rescue it now or cut your losses.

SOLUTION:

(Caution: The following can cause delight or depression.)

We are going to determine how many days you actually have left to deal with someday stuff. Sit down and calculate the number of years you most likely have left on this earth (the average man lives approximately seventy-four years; the average woman, eighty). Multiply that by fifty-two, the number of weeks in a year, and it will make you think in a perspective you never have. "Someday" doesn't stretch on forever—making someday *today* is the solution. After you've narrowed those piles and stacks down to the stuff you do still really want to get to, you know what to do, so start doing it *today*!

GOAL:

The reward for weeding down all that someday stuff: room for tomorrow!

For more on calling the bluff of do it "someday stuff," see Chapter 4 of *Clutter's Last Stand*, Chapter 7 of *For Packrats Only*, and Chapter 6 of *Clutter Free! Finally & Forever*.

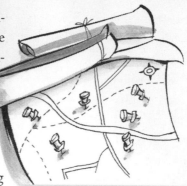

FARMED OUT WEIGHT

- It's yours, all right, but it's not at your place
- Clothes, cars, containers of clutter of all kinds kept or left at someone else's place

SUMMARY:

This dropped-off, left-behind, forgotten, or intentionally-stored-there stuff is someone else's to worry about and look after. (And it takes up and junks up their precious room, too.) It is unkind, obnoxious, and inconsiderate to leave our litter somewhere too long. Offering short-term storage to someone until he can reload or relocate is true charity, but this dislocated clutter gets old fast for those housing it, whether they are family, friends, or enemies! The worse the junk, the worse the irritation. Good family and friends will keep (neatly boxed) good stuff longer, but don't forget about it and don't forget to thank them.

For more on "mother load" clutter, see Chapter 7 of *For Packrats Only,* and Chapter 6 of *Clutter Free! Finally & Forever.*

SOLUTION:

Make a written list or chart of your invasions:

Inventory

What	Where It Is	Why	Since When	Disposition
Maternity/ baby stuff	At Mother's	We moved	20 years ago	I'm 65— guess I can give it away
My old Honda	The vacant lot at work	Transmission finally went	6 months ago	Call the junk dealer today!

If you are shocked by what you wrote in the first four columns of this chart, activate that last one right away. Too many of us shunt our excess onto others.

GOAL:

Don't let stuff you have stashed anywhere wear out its welcome (or, for that matter, yours!).

REAL ESTATE CLUTTER

- Extra land
- Extra lawn
- Extra home space
- Sheds
- Apartments
- Time-shares
- Vacation homes
- Speculation properties

. . . That you don't use.

SUMMARY:

We don't want all the land in the world, just all that borders us! Too many of us end up (through inheritance, remodeling, moving, upgrading, idle coveting, or just plain building a life and family or business) with too much property or land, which we hang on to for dear life. Take buildings, for instance. What once housed a family or earned a living is great, but when we outgrow it or no longer need something quite so big, it often stays to be cared for (cleaned and maintained and policed and taxed, etc.). Shelter can evolve to something to shepherd, and excess land can exhaust both your resources and your energy.

SOLUTION:

For landlock: List or lay out on paper all of the properties you own and honestly enter their status and forecast below.

In more than forty years of being responsible for real estate, I've owned a bunch of it, and the answer is to sell it if you're not using it or if you don't have a clear projected plan for it. Keeping property for investment purposes or enjoyment makes sense, but don't keep it just because you have it. Realtors will tell you that, too. The basis for judgment here is whether it is a delight and pleasure, a sound investment, a positive influence on you and others—or a drain. When you can't ride your range, put it to rest.

REAL ESTATE CODE (GOAL):

Not letting land or property put you under.

For more real estate reading, see Chapter 12 of *Clutter's Last Stand*, and page 61 of *For Packrats Only*.

Parcel or Property	Original Cost	Today's Value	Taxes	Payments	Interest	Time Period	Maintenance Costs	(Realistic) Future Value

VEHICLE CLUTTER

- Cars
- Trucks
- Vans
- Jeeps
- RVs
- SUVs
- Sports cars
- Go-karts
- Four-wheelers
- Motorcycles
- Motorbikes
- Snowmobiles
- Trailers
- Boats
- Tractors
- "Restorable," "repairable," and retired vehicles.

SUMMARY:

We've built our fleet, in a little over 100 years, from a mere means of transportation to vehicles that ease work and provide sport, romance, and excitement. There is a vehicle to fit almost every phase of our life, work, play, and ego. They're easy to buy, too, so even a person of modest means can easily end up with several vehicles to tend. Once, the average person owned a two-ton car. Now automobiles are smaller and lighter, and there are many different varieties of vehicle, so we often have two or more of them apiece. Maintaining all this—making the payments on them, insuring, protecting, cleaning and polishing them, and finding a place to store them (plus guilt about the ones we don't use enough to justify ownership of)—is weight indeed.

SOLUTION:

Vehicle clutter has two basic causes:

1. Too many cars. Spare shoes or hand tools are hard enough to tend, but a spare vehicle that gets limited or little use depreciates you even faster than it depreciates. Infrequently used vehicles; vehicles that were once used and now are not; vehicles that you're "going to restore/repair/rebuild someday"; and plain old junk cars around your place, your folks' place, the storage center, the lot next door, the backyard, or the back forty are nothing but clutter on wheels.

2. Too much car. Luxury is a silly word to connect with cars. Safety and soundness are one thing, but luxury (that $10,000, $20,000, or $30,000 extra you pay for trendy transportation) is a big and often unnecessary extra expense no matter how ingeniously you finance it. Are the few hours or minutes you spend daily in a car worth weeks and years of straining and stretching to pay for it? What about the loss of the better things you could do with that money? Vanity is one of life's largest weights, and vehicles reign as one of the top vanity victimizers (of men, especially).

The average car today can get you where you want and need to go, look neat and presentable, and be safe for 100,000 to 200,000 miles—even 300,000 miles. Keeping your present car as long as you can will save money, time, and the environment.

GOAL:

Being in the "driver's seat" again. Trading all that parking space for some room for personal growth.

For more on minimizing vehicle clutter, see Chapter 9 of *Clutter's Last Stand*, Chapter 6 of *For Packrats Only*, and Chapter 6 of *Clutter Free! Finally and Forever.*

PROTECTIVE CLUTTER

- Locks
- Keys
- Alarms
- Monitors
- Buzzers
- Guards
- Bars
- Fences
- Electric eyes
- Closed-circuit TV
- Security lights
- Safes
- Safety-deposit boxes
- Extra insurance on car, house, contents, and person (and insurance inventories)
- Mace, tear gas, guard dogs, guns

SUMMARY:

It's a real irony that we strive and save to buy a bunch of "good stuff," and then have so many expensive things that we need to own, rent, or lease a string of alarms, locks, safes, fences, guards, and electronics to protect them because we aren't there using them. All this protection gear takes up space, and it has to be installed, maintained, monitored, and paid for, and records have to be kept on it—for what? To guard our overload. People seldom steal the common everyday necessities—it's the luxury stuff that is always the target. The jewels or the paintings are too expensive to wear or show, so we hide them and pay for protectors to keep not us, but our stuff, out of danger. The result is that at work and at home, we spend about a quarter of our lives getting in and out of places.

SOLUTION:

Protection devices create more tension than peace of mind, as we are always worried about whether they are working right, and whether we have the best or right one.

The best self-protection (which is our ultimate goal) is having fewer possessions people will want to take from you. So walk through your inventory and list exactly what you are "guarding," and then beside each listed item write why you are guarding it. If the why is a good, sound reason, it's a keeper. If you have to think twice, it is generally something you might consider finding a new owner for.

GOAL:

Culling those "valuables" down to the things that are truly valuable to you. Carrying fewer keys, combinations, codes, and concealed apparatuses; having fewer code numbers, lights, and locks to worry about.

For more on security clutter, see Chapter 4 of *Clutter's Last Stand*.

- Parts
- Accessories and attachments to all kinds of things
- Construction scraps/leftovers
- Chemicals
- Broken items
- Seasonal stuff
- Trash and garbage
- Gardening goodies
- Sports equipment
- Cleaning gear
- Oils
- Solvents
- Rags
- Every tool coming and going
- Recycling inventory
- Drums and containers
- Second-best furniture
- Retired cars

GARAGE CLUTTER

SUMMARY:

Although the garage is often the largest open space on the home scene, it is the least wisely used. Seldom can a car get in. The garage offers us not only safe vehicle storage but space for active and creative projects. Yet we offer it piles of pathetic house and yard overflow. Truly, this is the "on its way out, but detained for further study" syndrome. Most garages offer an obstacle course of opportunities to trip and fall, plus a place for things to rot or receive damage. All of this is a sure source of a heated argument or two (or more).

SOLUTION:

First, you should simply and honestly remove all the *trash*! This includes things that are:

- Empty
- Dried up
- Hardened
- Broken
- Outdated
- Worn out
- Bottomless
- Unfixable
- Rejected (you never wanted it, or you have a better one)

Second, you should restore or reroute the rest:

- Sharpen the dull.
- Paint the ugly, peeling, or porous.
- Return the borrowed or pirated, and call the owners of anything else that isn't yours and tell them it's time for pickup.
- Relocate the things that don't fit here or belong somewhere else.
- Refinish or repair things in need of it, and move them back into the house.

Third, mount or cover anything you can. Any way you can get "it" (a worthwhile, legitimate garage inhabitant) off the floor, do it—shelve it, hang it, put in a closet or cabinet. Clear off that concrete!

Fourth, if it is unfinished, seal the floor using the following steps:

1. Buy a can of clear concrete seal.
2. Clean and prepare the floor following the instructions on the can, and then coat the entire floor with seal and let it dry well. This will give you a shiny, smooth surface to drive, walk, and work on. Pet droppings, oil drips, and spills can be removed, and project mess swept up, in seconds.

The garage is the first area you see when you get home and the most direct route into your house. When clean, it will not only give you a lift, but it will prevent stains and litter from drifting into the house.

GOAL:

Have room for the car and to-do projects, without having

to clear away and rearrange things.

For more on de-garbaging the garage, see Chapter 5 of *Clutter's Last Stand*, pages 82–83 of *Make Your House Do the Housework*, page 60 of *For Packrats Only*, and pages 145–146 of *Clutter Free! Finally & Forever*.

OUTDOOR CLUTTER

- Parked or porched toys
- Tools
- Tires
- Rusted iron and steel
- Scraps and torn-out stuff from remodeling jobs and do-it-yourself projects
- Old flowerpots and potting supplies
- Abandoned vehicles and vehicle parts
- Bags and sacks
- Rotting firewood
- Old doghouses

- Defunct bird feeders
- Sagging swing sets
- Leaning sheds
- Failing fences
- Dead lawn mowers and appliances
- Litter and garbage
- Deteriorated yard decorations
- Dead bushes
- Fallen tree branches
- Parts
- More parts
- Packaging
- Evicted furniture

SUMMARY:

First impressions, and even final judgments about our character and housekeeping, are made before anyone ever meets us or enters our home. Our grounds give us away and can keep respect, pride, and efficiency away, too. Trash outside hints at more of the same inside.

SOLUTION:

Mother Nature is not going to remove most of this, so:

1. Contain. Have nothing out or loose that will clutter up the place, blow around, or be attractive to thieves or dangerous to children. Just

have the real useful, used, and weatherproof items out there. Keep dust and mud-producing dirt covered with vegetation, and dead or broken parts of trees and bushes pruned or picked up.

2. Refrain. The yard is not a place to stash or store things. Weather and exposure take a big toll, so anything outside has an ongoing price tag with a big "to do" on it. Limit what you put out there and you won't have to be constantly painting, repainting, covering up, taking in and out, retrieving, tying down, etc.

3. Maintain. Trade some of your exercise equipment for an active yard care/scouting session. Grounds need regular policing to remain junk-free.

GOAL:

Not having to endure—coming or going—anything resembling an obstacle course. Eliminating any visual pollution, as well as the need to make excuses or apologies for the condition of your grounds. Making any outside space you own into an attractive place to play ball, sniff flowers, or roll in the grass.

For more on ousting outdoor clutter, see Chapters 4, 5, and 11 of *Clutter's Last Stand*, Chapters 6 and 7 of *For Packrats Only*, and pages 137–138 of *Clutter Free! Finally & Forever*.

KIDS' CLUTTER

- Papers
- Crayons
- Stuffed animals
- Play sets
- Cribs
- Chairs
- Fast-food fallout
- Balls
- Bats
- Strollers
- Kiddie care gear and car gear
- Books
- Dolls
- Pets
- Outgrown clothes
- Outgrown video games and equipment
- Toys, toys, toys
- Toy boxes

There are at least 6,000 categories of child clutter!

SUMMARY:

One kid today has more stuff than an entire kindergarten would have had a few years ago. The source of all this is both heredity and environment, or in other words, us—the adults of all ages who lugged all this in and laid it on our kids. A very high percentage of kiddie clutter is things bought to please and appease kids, often as a substitute for time spent with them. The choice here is to lose the clutter, or you'll lose the kid (in more ways than one) in it.

SOLUTION:

1. Give it a place. Kids' stuff especially needs to have a designated area for it to be containable. If there isn't a specific place or space to park it when the playing is over for the day, then out with it. Overflow will always be underfoot.
2. De-duplicate. Double and triple of everything is a great way to spoil kids and teach them indecision and waste. And remember that replacing any broken thing and refilling every toy vacancy are not child-raising requirements.
3. Retreat—from offers of extra gifts, trips, and places that have a big take-home souvenir price tag.

GOAL:

Save your *children*, rather than all the stuff that will only spoil and confuse them or warp their values. Their hands can be better occupied than with a game controller, and where there is less clutter there will be less nagging, yelling, arguing, and little kiddie fights.

For more on controlling kiddie clutter, see Chapter 5 of *Clutter's Last Stand*, Chapter 15 of *For Packrats Only*, and Chapter 6 of *Clutter Free! Finally & Forever*.

PET CLUTTER

- Cages
- Collars
- Leashes
- Chains
- Toys
- Tags
- Dishes and feeders and leftover food by the broken sack
- Pills, powders, and pharmaceutical potions
- Kitty beds and doggie quilts
- Grooming tools
- Pedigrees
- Training aids
- Shampoos
- Leads
- Saddles
- Harnesses
- Chains
- Litter-handling devices
- Stained containers
- Abandoned aquariums complete with mossy castles, blue gravel, and a broken pump

SUMMARY:

Pets are meant to bless, not mess up, our lives. The time, space, and money to keep pets and all of their paraphernalia are well spent if they give us pleasure. (And there are pets whose personality surpasses that of most humans in the household.) The "burden" of pets is often not the pets themselves, but all the excess trappings and supplies we accumulate while the pet is with us, or the stuff we keep long after the pet is gone. Active articles are all right—it is the obsolete, the duplicates, the unused, and the nonworking that become the tail that wags the dog.

SOLUTION:

1. Centralizing pet supplies and accessories (and maybe even the pets themselves) to certain areas of the house and grounds can do a lot to cut down on pet clutter.

2. Trash (or sell or pass on) all the duplicates; ruined, outgrown, or retired things; and the "didn't work" or "wouldn't eat" items.

3. Don't keep paraphernalia for pets you're no longer

interested in, or if both the pet and those who loved the pet are gone!

4. Point out the burden of pet overload to the owner of the pet, if it happens not to be you.

5. Resist ever getting a pet that you aren't going to stay interested in and be willing to invest the time and trouble to take care of.

STUPID STUFF

GOAL:

Something to bark, crow, and chirp about—less pet mess. Have more room for Rover, less stain and odor, less hunting for things, and fewer heated discussions.

For more on minimizing pet mess, see page 88 of *For Packrats Only*, and *Pet Clean-Up Made Easy, 2nd Edition*—a fun guide to every aspect of pet mess cleanup and prevention.

- Screws from ankle surgery
- Wad of stuck-together stamps
- Twenty years' worth of wishbones
- Dead cactus complete with pot
- Bale of hay in basement
- Your ex-wife's nail polish
- Leopard-skin patterned water heater made into a chair
- A pirated "No U-Turn" sign
- The cast that was removed from your cat's broken leg
- Crate of cordovan shoe polish
- Bladeless fan
- Bald snow tires
- Broken baby tooth
- Pet snake's shed skin
- Shelf ornament made out of a moose dropping
- Half-melted mushroom-shaped candle

You get the idea.

SUMMARY:

We often don't even know why we are keeping things like this—maybe on a dare, to irritate someone else, because we are not 100 percent sure what it is, or maybe we think we may be able to use it to spark conversation. Or maybe we just never thought about it.

Stupid stuff is really of no use or value to anyone, and it gives us bad vibes. Yet we have kept it and are still keeping it. It doesn't have a chance of becoming an antique; it's not even good for a laugh anymore. One or two stupid things keep us humble; the other forty-six we can surely do without.

SOLUTION:

1. This is one case where it is okay to let others express their opinion of your junk, and you listen to them.
2. Pass stupid stuff on to a new generation of jokers if they show any interest in it.
3. Display and offer it at a "stupid party" (especially if drinks are being served).
4. You can, of course, just trash it!

GOAL:

Keep only the stuff that has some class or some purpose. Make sure anything of this type that you keep has some redeeming value for you or others, and that you do have the space to accommodate it (stupid space).

For more secrets of shucking real stupid stuff, see any chapter of my other books on dejunking.

OTHERS' CLUTTER

- **Anything covered in this book, except that it is someone else's, not yours**
- **Habits, hardware, soft goods, or general mess**

SUMMARY:

Many people have written me over the years about how their mother or father or friend, etc., "does not see the mess" that he or she is living in. It may be total chaos and squalor, and yet the person sees absolutely nothing amiss.

"I've begun to declutter in spite of my husband's valiant effort to protect 60 pairs of shoes, 84 pairs of socks, 75 collected caps, and sets of 1936 law books. . . . I'm not perfect, but compared to him. . . . "

When someone else's stuff is out of control, it often goes out of bounds and infringes on our territory—affects our nerves, pocketbook, and flexibility. We end up carrying some of that person's weight and we don't like it. Until that person loses his or her excess, we, in subtle or not-so-subtle ways, are abused and embarrassed by it (people may avoid visiting, make sarcastic comments, etc.). This is not something we want to face forever—we'll do it for our own clutter, maybe, but not for someone else's. And we prefer not to use the rock-bottom alternatives, such

as leaving, torching the pile, or getting a divorce.

SOLUTION:

None of the following work, so save your energy: threatening, intimidating, nagging, criticizing, serving notice, preaching, plundering their stash, or demanding that they get rid of all this, or else! Even if something is cursed and disliked by the owner himself, just try to take it away from him and you would think he was losing his birthright.

What does work?

1. Avoid cluttered situations and people in the first place.
2. Let the person know (in a low-key, loving way) that you really don't like it.
3. Limit her area. Most people respect boundaries when they're clearly spelled out. Confine the space and you may confine the stuff.
4. Be a perfect example of clutter-free living yourself. Say with actions (not words!), "Look at all the room I have, Harry." Good example is and always will be the most effective approach.

Exposing someone long and subtly enough to a squared-away life is likely to eventually ignite a spark of understanding that living clutter-free is living better. And when he does alter his cluttering course, he'll know what to do because of what he has seen.

5. Praise, admire, and compliment any improvements she makes.

"One thing that is helping the cause is including my husband in the dejunking decisions. He's still a packrat, but I think all he wanted in the past was to be in the loop. I'll fill up a box and show it to him. It's amazing how little he actually pulls out to keep. And this is the man who stashed a lawnmower in our living room several years ago."

GOAL:

To somehow motivate the other person or other people to clear away the clutter so you can find each other, often for the first time!

For more sane solutions to others' clutter, see Chapters 14 and 16 of *For Packrats Only*, and Chapter 6 of *Clutter Free! Finally & Forever*; see also Chapter 6 of *The Office Clutter Cure*.

Needed:
Inventions and Tools to Assist Clutter Sufferers

* Pile X-ray
* Clutter carbon dater (as the little prongs or suction cups make contact, it analyzes, ages, weighs, and dates things)
* Clutter wallpaper (you can see and savor it all, but not have to dust it or deal with it in any way)
* A bottomless shopping bag (so that whatever is put in there never makes it home)

Chapter 7

Room-by-Room Guide to Clutter

Whether it's the mountain range outside our window or grease spatters on our range, the longer something is there, the less we see it. This is even more true of the stuff that gradually fills all the surfaces and spaces of our home sweet home—clutter! Even the most experienced wildlife watcher often needs an experienced guide to see all that is worth seeing. Let me be that spotter for you now.

Kitchen

Top of Refrigerator

Does whatever is up here really need to be out collecting dust and grime? Do you use it often, or does it for some reason deserve permanent display? If it was originally edible, how long ago did you forget it was here?

Inside Refrigerator

You can always find clutter (things you never really use, or that should be graduated to the compost pile) in here. Check carefully the backs of all shelves, any shelves or covered storage compartments on the door, and those lower vegetable bins. Refrigerator space is always at a premium, so why would you want to surrender any of it to things like the opened can of anchovies Aunt Ida left behind, a bottle of key lime juice gone gray, jars with a single pickle left floating in them, those mini jars of mustard that came in a food gift basket (which no one is ever willing to try or to throw away), aged packets of fast-food chain condiments, or the two-pound jar of maraschino cherries you lost your head and bought several years ago?

Freezer

Out with anything that's been in here more than a year, including those little treasures like the fish head you were saving for bait, the frozen egg yolks you never remember to use, those chicken gizzards that are supposed to be such a gourmet treat, and the remains of the smoked turkey you tried and didn't like. Remember—freezing things doesn't preserve them forever, and it definitely doesn't improve them.

Back of the Stove

Relocate those spices you don't use all the time, empty saltboxes, and grease spots and stains.

Spice Racks

When we buy a bottle or can of spice, we tend to think of it as a lifetime investment, but most spices lose much of their flavor and savor after two to five years, and some even sooner. Just because you still have the little jar of red pepper you bought in Albuquerque fifteen years ago doesn't mean it would do anything for the chili now. Review and renew—it'll improve the next stew.

Counters

Keep the kitchen looking good and working space clear by ruthlessly decluttering your counters. There are usually plenty of unworthy squatters on them, such as the following:

- Rarely or never-used small appliances
- Old newspapers
- Piles of mail and other paper junk
- Canisters and like containers filled with things you never get around to using (e.g., glass jars full of aged poppy seed or rancid sesame seed oil)
- Crocks bristling with plastic, wooden, and metal utensils, some of which you're not even sure what they are

Whatnot (or Junk) Drawer

This is the drawer usually full of stuff it would be neat to use but which we never do:

- Corn holders complete with corn silk brush
- Cannoli molds
- Nutmeg grater
- Lobster cracking kit for six
- Cherry pitter
- Strawberry huller
- Melon baller
- Aluminum nails for baked potatoes
- At least six packs of bamboo skewers that we keep buying and keep forgetting to use

Plus, of course, there are those good old odds and ends:

- Used birthday candles
- Cheap broken sunglasses
- Nonworking cigarette lighters
- A few marbles
- Five boxes of plastic forks
- Plugs of cotton from pill bottles
- The opened package of valentine doilies you bought for a bridal shower umpteen years ago
- A half-dozen fuses (you now have only breakers)
- At least three toothpick holders and boxes of toothpicks

Some of these whatnots we actually do use from time to time—get those better organized and move out the rest.

Upper Cupboards

These unfortunately misused areas are frequently the home of gifts not quite to our taste and impulse buys from "culinary complication" stores:

- Pasta maker
- Device for making apple-shaped cutouts in pie crust
- Casserole we never use, complete with charming custom-fitted wooden hotplate
- Heart-shaped cake pans and Easter candy molds that never make it out of the cupboard
- Enough extra cups and mugs to serve coffee to a convention

Lower Cupboards

- Heavyweight stuff we inherited from someone, oversize stuff, bowls we never use

- Forgotten appliances (such as the second mixer and the juicer that churned out carrot juice for all of two weeks after we got it)

Under the Sink

Usually crowded with aged, rusted, spilling, water-damaged cleaning supplies of all kinds, many of which we never use and some of which we shouldn't. The contents of many of these bottles, boxes, cans, and jars are poisonous, too. Replace all of this with a few professional cleaning chemicals that work better and cost less—see the questions on this in *Do I Dust or Vacuum First? 2nd Edition*, or Chapter 5 of *Is There Life After Housework? 2nd Edition*.

Hutch or China Cabinet

Usually inhabited by the following likely disposables:

- Second and third sets of dishes and silverware
- Place mats and cloth napkins that have never made it to the table
- A little-too-much-of-a-novelty china
- Ornate things you never use and may not even like

Lower Shelves of Microwave Stand or Other Stands

If you look carefully enough here you will find:

- Chewed-up rubber toys deposited here by the family dog
- Stained place mats
- The accessories to a mixer you no longer have
- Stacks of foil cake and pie tins

- The hammer and screwdriver you haven't been able to find
- A lot of dirt and dust!

Bulletin Board

Anything here that has turned yellow or is announcing something that took place last year can safely be considered clutter.

Crevices Between Countertop and Stove

Items in places like this have usually fallen or been forgotten here. Dejunk yourself of old, warped cutting boards and cookie sheets, trays you never use, and the leaf to a long-departed table.

Walls or Ceiling

Kitchen walls and ceilings collect an amazing amount of airborne grease from cooking, so it's a good idea to limit the number of places for it to collect. Get rid of those:

- Hanging plants that have been hung until dead
- Pots and pans and aspic molds you dust but don't use
- Framed mottos and sayings that are no longer as charming or funny as they were years ago when you first hung them

"Don't you just love those matching moose salt and pepper shakers and napkin holder, and that plaque with 'God Bless America' spelled out in split

peas? The shellacked string of garlic was a little
better before all the garlic shriveled up."

Porch or Mud Room

Floor by the Door

Of the at least eighteen pairs of shoes and boots here, how
many still fit? And are still in good repair? Don't just shuffle
the lame and the halt back to the closet—get rid of them.

Clothes Hooks

Usually at least a third of what is hanging here includes
defunct or nonfunctional garments:

- Too-small snowsuits
- The woolen vest you won't wear
- The beat-up sweater someone left behind
- The giant shawl you used when you were pregnant
- Out-of-favor baseball caps
- Raincoats that don't deflect the drops anymore
- Coveralls/overalls so full of holes they no longer
  cover all

Jumbo Junk

Jumbo junk really limits the use of a porch or mud room
and doesn't do much for appearance, either. You can't miss
these items:

- The giant crock you bought with visions of making
  sauerkraut, which mainly serves now as a convenient

place to stash unworn scarves, worn-out gloves, torn galoshes, and broken umbrellas
- The trim left over from remodeling
- The big piece of Formica that was cut out of the sink hole
- That nonworking dehumidifier
- The 250-pound fireplace insert
- The old wringer washer you rescued from a neighbor's curb and haven't decided what to do with

Seasonal Stowaways

Things like this are often a sign that the alleged storage place of the items in question is too inconvenient:

- The canning jars and kettle that never made it back to the basement
- The plant starter trays and half bag of vermiculite left here when you finished with them five months ago
- The netting that covered the cherry tree last spring
- The storm windows/screens you took out, which are almost due to go back in
- Air conditioners
- Fans
- Snow shovels
- The Christmas lights that were taken down but are still lying in a heap in the corner of the porch

Pet Clutter

If you're not sure what to do with your pet messes and clutter, check out my book on the subject, *Pet Clean-Up Made Easy, 2nd Edition*. Some of the more obvious items you should steer clear of keeping:

- The bag of food the dog wouldn't eat
- The cat self-feeder or kitten condo you don't use any-more
- The litter pan you don't need anymore
- An empty lime-encrusted aquarium
- The dog tie-out chain and stake your college-age son left behind on his last visit

Stuff En Route to Somewhere

Examine all such stuff carefully—if it's been sitting there for quite a while, maybe it should simply be eliminated. Then establish a clear-cut location (such as a big sturdy box) for things on their way to the cellar or garage, to be taken back to the toolbox or to the store, or wherever. If there's no doubt from now on as to what's supposed to be moving out, you'll be more likely to take it with you on your way.

Sift through:

- That pile of clothes that was supposed to go to the dry cleaner
- That bag of sewing scraps
- Those empty bottles you were going to add to your collection in the shed
- The dead plants that were supposed to be dumped

Living Room

Shelves, Mantels, Shadowboxes, etc.

Which of the little objects perched here are still a pleasure to look at and a pride to own, and which would you be just as happy to not have to dust and protect from little visitors anymore?

Bookcases

Look out for books that are serving mainly as shelf dressing (see the section on books in Chapter 6). Don't forget all that long-forgotten stuff on top of the bookcase and stacked sideways in any space left above the books on the shelves.

End Tables

If they have drawers or any kind of storage space inside, it will usually be filled with:

- Dog-eared paperbacks
- Outdated phone books
- Pens that don't write
- Forgotten needlework projects
- The set of photos you were looking for everywhere
- The *AAA Guide to Lake Cumberland 1989*

Walls

Free your wall space of:

- Pictures, paintings, etc., you never really liked but were a gift or simply filled a blank space over the couch
- Wall decorations that look tacky to you now (such as those little heart-shaped shelves filled with knick-knacks, or that pair of plaster of Paris mallards in flight)

Audio and Video Clutter

The living room or family room is prime habitat for techno-clutter, a species that multiplies wildly and goes extinct quickly. So be on the lookout for:

- CDs and tapes you should never have bought
- Things you shouldn't have bothered to record
- Borrowed tapes
- Damaged tapes (quit kidding yourself that you're going to somehow thread all that back in or that it would still sound or look the same if you did)
- CDs and tapes you never listen to anymore
- Speakers to a sound system you no longer have
- Nonworking remotes
- The old "rabbit ears" TV antenna you no longer need
- The extra coil of wire you bought when you were thinking of adding a third TV
- Ancient record-cleaning kits
- Awful scratched CDs you bought at a garage sale

Magazine Rack

(See section on magazines in Chapter 6.)

China Closet or Hutch

Do you truly need any of this stuff?

- The silver you polish occasionally but never use
- Vases and candy dishes so fancy you're afraid to ever put them out
- The food warmer your sister got for her wedding and didn't want and that you don't really want either
- Never-used wineglasses, rice bowls, platters, trays, and hors d'oeuvre dishes

"My cousin considers a room undressed without a solid lining of furniture on every wall, and after she visits a secondhand store or auction, will often get started on a second row all around."

Bedroom

Under the Bed

Be alert here for both official and unofficial under-bed storage:

- Plastic or cardboard boxes of neat stuff we probably shouldn't have bothered to keep
- Ties to robes we no longer have
- Worn-out slippers
- Lost balls and cat toys
- The bag of clothes someone gave us that we meant to go through

Upper Shelves and Floor of Closet

(See section on closets in Chapter 6.)

Clothes in Closet

(See section on clothes in Chapter 6.)

Top of Chest of Drawers

Most of what ends up on here ought to go in the top drawer of the dresser but doesn't because that drawer is filled up with never-worn bow ties and the box to every watch you ever bought or received as a gift (see following section).

Inside Dresser

You want your drawers to neatly hold your nicely folded clothing. Instead, you've got:

- Gift wallets you'll never use
- Fancy hankies still in their original gift boxes
- Bows from old Christmas/birthday packages
- Three or four travel sewing kits and sets of manicure tools
- Glasses cases too small for the kind of glasses you wear now
- Single gloves
- Removed shoulder pads from clothes you no longer wear
- Pajamas/nightgowns of types you will never wear again
- Lost-its-scent sachet
- Antique lingerie (such as girdles, garter belts, and shapeless yellowed bras)
- Old bathing suits that would never fit now

- An entire drawer full of hair ties and barrettes, of which you've worn no more than three or four times

Top of Dresser

Like most surfaces, we've got all kinds of things we don't need stacked and stored and falling off of our dresser:

- Ancient bottles of perfume and cologne
- Fancy brushes and combs that don't really do the job well
- Never-used boxes of powder and powder puffs
- Q-tips everywhere but in the dispenser

Night Table

The night table is another unfortunate victim, just like the top of the dresser. It usually houses things like:

- Heating pads that never make it beyond lukewarm
- Nonworking alarm clocks
- Eyeglasses from several prescriptions ago
- Burned-out nightlights
- Ineffective insomnia aids
- Books you started and couldn't bring yourself to finish
- Incomplete decks of cards
- Several almost-empty tubes of muscle and joint rub
- Aged cold remedies and other medicines

Headboard Junk

If you are unlucky enough to have a headboard with little storage shelves in it, it will probably be inhabited by the close relatives of night table junk.

Jewelry Box

A jewelry box is a place to store jewelry and keep it clean and orderly. Relieve it of all the items that will impede this:

- Jewelry you've outgrown
- Broken jewelry
- Orphaned earrings and single cufflinks and the like
- Expensive jewelry you rarely wear and are tired of guarding

Hall

Hall Table

If there is any kind of horizontal surface in a hall, it will be filled with things people need to get rid of in a hurry and can't be bothered to put where they belong. So the table itself is worth questioning.

Linen Closet

Just because something can be folded and stuffed on a shelf doesn't mean it's worth keeping. Ream through here for things like:

- Threadbare tea towels
- Fitted sheets for sizes of beds you don't have
- One-of-a-kind pillowcases

- Runners you never use
- Tablecloths that don't fit any table you have
- Gift linens still in their original boxes
- Ruined throw rugs
- The doilies you can't be bothered to iron and starch
- The toilet seat cover that never stayed on
- Ugly old worn-out shower curtains

Coat Closet

Coat closets are always overcrowded because hanger for hanger, the unused garments in here are much bulkier than other kinds of clothes clutter. And we're extra reluctant to part with them because we paid so much for them once. (See "Clothes Clutter" in Chapter 6.) Get tough here and make some space for the coats and jackets you *really* use now.

Bathroom

Sink/Counter

This bathroom surface usually needs to be purged of things like:

- Worn-out toothbrushes
- Down-to-the-last-sliver bars of soap
- The soft-soap dispenser that won't pump anymore
- Overused disposable razors
- Never-finished bottles of hair products
- Never-used cans of Bag Balm
- The pills that didn't get put away
- Several extra brushes or combs

Vanity Drawers

Just like our dresser drawers, drawers in a vanity are often almost half full of junk, such as:

- Tubes of stuff with only one more squeeze in them
- Lotions so old they are either dried up or beyond any kind of medicinal action
- Wrong-shade makeup
- Stomach-settling medicine that dates back to '92
- Electric shavers no one uses anymore
- Aged anti-aging remedies
- Rusty bobby pins
- Set of nine fake fingernails
- The extra jars of Vicks you bought by mistake
- Miniature soaps, shower caps, and shoe polishing cloths from at least eight different hotels
- That hair-removing machine you used for thirty seconds once

Under the Bathroom Sink

A scene very similar to what you find under the kitchen sink, except that the aged chemicals here are mostly beauty, health, and grooming aids such as:

- Shampoos, mousses, and gels we tried and didn't like
- The conditioner that always makes our scalp break out
- The brand of tampons we don't use anymore
- That box of Epsom salts and the giant jug of mineral oil that've been down there forever

Often lurking here, too, are things like:

- Worn-out toilet brushes
- Bargain toilet paper that feels like sandpaper

Medicine Cabinet

This small space is usually packed with:

- Ancient prescriptions (your medical history at a glance)
- Antique Ex-Lax
- Antediluvian eye drops
- Combs with missing teeth
- Dried-up nail polish
- Hardened facial masks
- Aged vitamins and minerals
- Several Band-Aid boxes with one bandage left in each
- The bottle of witch hazel no one has ever opened

No medicine cabinet made is big enough for an over-the-counter (OTC) junker. The OTC junker needs one shelf for cold remedies, one for headache remedies, one for stomach remedies, one for foot remedies, and one for skin emollients. How could you squander any space on first-aid supplies when you have to shelve all this?

Outside

Front of House Clutter

The inside of your house will be judged by whatever people see in front of your house! Clean up, throw out, or put away:

- Toys, toys, toys (including broken, rusted, sun-faded, and outgrown toys)
- The snow shovel you left outside last winter
- That plastic swan, cement goose, or bronze raccoon that doesn't look so cute to you anymore

Outside the Back Door

Same rules apply to the back door as apply to the front of the house. Discard:

- That pile of scraps and torn-out things from your remodeling project
- Buckets with holes in them
- The scorched pan you set outside in a big hurry one day
- All the things you decluttered but didn't dispose of (see Chapter 6)

Porch/Patio Clutter

These areas are here for your enjoyment, but you can't even find a place to sit among all the:

- Cracked flowerpots and rotted flower boxes
- Abandoned couches
- Plants that should be put out to pasture
- Nonworking thermometers
- No-good watering cans
- Picnic tables with mushrooms growing out of them
- Old, rusty broken glider and the old wicker chair no one will sit on for fear of falling through

Window Wells

Everything in here (except the marble chips and visiting toad) is probably clutter.

Fenceline Clutter

This is an area that, when clean, can really add to the charm of your home. There's no need to leave:

- Last year's leaves in big plastic bags
- That pile of firewood you salvaged even though you don't have a woodstove
- Ratty old rugs someone hung on the fence
- All that litter that blew up against the posts

Past Pet Clutter

Things we bought or built to accommodate a bird or animal usually lack the charm of the creature itself, especially when these trappings are well past their prime or long neglected. So evict things like:

- Decrepit doghouses
- Rabbit hutches and pigeon coops that are beyond repair or you'll never use again
- That broken birdbath
- The hummingbird feeder missing five of its six "blossoms"

Open Spaces Clutter

Don't you miss your wide-open spaces? It's time to trash:

- Outgrown kiddie pools
- Sandless sandboxes
- Outgrown swing sets
- Abandoned clotheslines
- Old broken-down fences
- Collapsing sheds

- The junk car that's never been hauled away
- The hedge you meant to remove
- The shrub that now overshadows the house

Chapter 8
To Keep It Off Now!

Preventing future clutter is the most important step of all in your decluttering campaign. How many of us have dieted with some success, and then seen the weight come creeping back slowly but surely? When it comes to a clutter diet (which at least as many of us go on each year), if we're not careful, within five years we'll have 150 percent of that excess back in our bins again.

So our final success in freeing ourselves from clutter is tied to what we do—or don't—pick back up the next weekend.

One of the biggest problems with those hell-bent to live free of junk and clutter is that they make dejunking a one-night stand—slam, bam, thank you garbage can. Then they forget clutter until it starts to fester again. Losing is about half of any decluttering project; keeping it lost is the other half. Clutter is not an "I got rid of it" process; it is more like a constant affliction you need to keep beating back: "I'm a clutter-holic, surrounded and tempted by it hourly, if not every second."

〜〜〜〜〜〜〜〜〜〜〜〜〜〜〜〜〜〜〜〜〜〜〜〜〜

"You asked how my house decluttering was going? I killed the beast, only to find out it had resurrected. Yes, I've learned that whatever I feed will grow!

"I bought a farmhouse from a woman of seventy-five, and it was filled with junk—balls of string, empty plastic bags, and tons of other stuff. It took a full year to get it cleaned out. I was horrified the whole time. The most horrible thing, however, was that within three months I had totally refilled it (and I moved there from an apartment)."

〜〜〜〜〜〜〜〜〜〜〜〜〜〜〜〜〜〜〜〜〜〜〜〜〜

Slipping back into clutter after we've overcome it is just as awful as going back to nursing a cigarette or gnawing on our cuticles. Sliding back, regaining old discarded habits—habits we were very happy to be relieved of—really hurts. So let's not even consider refilling our garage, drawers, closets, and other catacombs once we've decluttered them.

So what can we do to KEEP clutter gone now?

Don't Just Weed It Out; Get Rid of It

Make sure that when you say good-bye to junk, it's a clean, clear, definite "Good-bye," not "See you later, stuffed alligator." "Going" is seldom as good as "gone."

Operate Current

Don't let things pile up—try to deal with them as soon as they turn up. Keep active stuff; shun the passive.

Actively Dodge and Avoid Clutter

One thing about those pounds of ugly excess, nowadays we don't have to go after them, because of that magic thing called marketing. Every other time we pick up the phone, we find ourselves being talked into a product or service that was nowhere on our list of things to look into next. Catalogs for things we don't need and wouldn't have sought out jam our mailboxes, and TV, radio, and our time online are full of dramatic ads for more. Door-to-door solicitors, amateur and professional, and friends pushing some line of products accost us every time we turn around.

> A home full of clutter (like love or hate, wealth or poverty, leadership or following) is the result of many efforts, decisions, and actions over time. Clutter is like a glacier—you never see its mass move, but eventually it quietly smothers all in its path.

The bottom line is you can't just be a passive dejunker these days—you've got to be actively alert for clutter, constantly dodging and avoiding it. "Too much" doesn't arrive all at once. Clutter is rarely the result of one big event or one big mistake. It comes in a little at a time: a *little* picking up of *little* things at *little* shops for *little* reasons. . . . This totals up to *big* results in the end, and we end up with a lot of extra junk around the house.

As one man put it, "I can't remember buying more than a few suits, and I have forty-one suits now, and that's not counting the ones at the other house." Stay alert and on your guard: Every "little" act and purchase counts!

Think Before You Buy or Charge

"Why did I do that?" We ask ourselves this question a lot, don't we? Even me—I'm well educated, street smart, steeped in the subject of clutter, and a great giver of advice. Last month, I visited a major city on a convention trip. I already have a dozen sweatshirts in the closet, and I won't pay 99 cents for a glass of juice when water is available. Yet I forked out $39.95 for a sweatshirt that was just a $9.95 shirt with some silly local logo on it.

"Easy come, easy go" is more like "easy come, easy stay."

I heard someone the other day, living under the stress of debts, divorce, and doubts about the future (and extremely frustrated with all she had to handle), telling a group with great humor the only way out of this low was to get some therapy—"retail therapy." For some reason, people feel better when they shop. The results, however, eventually add to the problems that caused the need for retail therapy in the first place—not to mention all the clutter added. Is the pleasure of purchasing worth the pain (and it will be a pain) of paying for things, taking care of them, and then disposing of them?

Junk control—watching where you are going—saves lots of digging out from where you've been.

Think! One Head, Two Feet

Contingency planning is smart and economical, and duplicates of some things do make sense, for convenience, backup protection, or reasonable rotation. Even triplicates in things like shirts and skirts can be a good idea, but don't fall into the mindless multiplication trap. Something may be "cheaper by the dozen," but that doesn't mean you should stock up to the load limit—keeping something means cost and caring for it. Real security is in minimum, not maximum, these days. Why use your life up sustaining things you don't use?

Even One May Be Too Much

Often we think "too much" is a matter of multiplication—more than one, or too many of something. But as a young executive I know once pointed out, "I have too many boats . . . I have one." We don't necessarily have a right to, or need for, even one of everything. "None" is often a wonderful and sane solution.

You may be able to pay for it, but can you afford it?

Years ago, when we had less, many things might indeed have been nice to have. But today, with walls and halls, closets and clothes drawers, minds and garages bulging with excess, maybe we've finally reached the point where it would be nice *not* to have. . . .

"Consider the Source"

When I was in high school, the expression above was what you used to put down or discredit any nonsense laid on you. One would consider the source of the statement or the item, equate it with worthless, and dismiss it.

A leading advertiser told me that every one of us is bombarded (up to hundreds of times a day) with offers and suggestions from all kinds of avenues, inviting us to feel, touch, take, buy, smell, weigh, handle, borrow, try, taste, etc. Those messages are all meant to sell us something and get us to let loose of our time and money . . . and we do. Most of us, without hesitation, will take and keep a product, a recipe, a view, an idea from someone who has absolutely no qualifications regarding it or knowledge of what they are endorsing or advertising. We let them contribute to our "too much" solely because they are famous. How subtle these enticements can be, too. I was watching an Olympic race on TV once, and the announcers were expertly analyzing and projecting as the well-publicized runners rounded the last stretch. As one of the favorite athletes pulled in front of the pack near the finish line, the announcer rejoiced and excitedly said, "Well, folks, he has one Mercedes in the parking lot; now, he can line up another!" How innocently a remark like this indicates the reward for winning or achieving anything of merit—not only having the best, but adding extra. How does one drive two Mercedes?

Watch Out for Those Lying Labels

"Low fat," "less cholesterol," "lite beer," "limited numbers," tell us nothing, because if the subject is that insidious "too much," then lower, less, lighter, or limited is still excess and a punisher of your person!

Socially acceptable or popular is not a sancti-fier, either. Labels like "the cutting edge," "cool," "mature," "fashionable," or "pop-ular" don't add up to desirable.

Advertisers and copywriters have a whole vocabulary of button-pushing words they use to get us to reach for our credit cards or checkbooks. In the color insert ad from a popular elec-tronics firm, for example, I noticed all of the following "must have" words used in describing the different products and models:

"Great buy"

"Special"

"Most wanted"

"Get the second one for a penny"

"Fun maker"

"Mini handheld"

"Add to your . . ."

"Super selection"

"Bonus"

"Everyone needs . . ."

"Portable"

"Whole system"

"Bargain"

"Upgrade"

Another phrase to be wary of: "As seen on TV." How being on TV amounts to total sanctification for people I'll never know, but it has an almost unquestioned credibility. I will be somewhere mingling with the crowd like any other guest, and someone says, "He's been on TV!" Suddenly I'm a celebrity.

Before your next rush to get a pen and paper in the aftermath of a power ad on the tube, take a hard, objective look at all the rest of what is "on TV." You'll probably come to your senses. Take "on TV" as a warning, not a seal of approval.

Forget What Others Are Doing

Quit doing things because others do them, going along with the gang, ordering when and what they order. Select your own sources of consumption and entertainment; question who says it when you hear that something is a "must have," a "must see," or a "must buy."

Don't Look and You Won't Get Took

"Just browsing"—what good has ever come of browsing (unless you're a cow or deer)? Think about it: When you spend time checking out and hanging around a neat boutique or new car showroom, you're just plain cruising for a choosing. Browsing is the sire of buying, and you're soon not just getting what you don't need, but the best of what you don't need.

Between interviews in New York one day, for example, I ran down to the street during lunch to pick up some Scotch tape and a ruler in the only store nearby. It turned out to be an "odds and ends" shop, and had everything under the sun except tape and rulers. The aisles were so packed that you couldn't move—you had to wait for a surge or a flow in the direction you hoped to go. There were scores of people in there in a buying frenzy. Since the merchandise was of every imaginable kind, most of those browsers were probably there just for something to do to kill time. People were pawing through total trash, squeezing, patting, and stretching things to test some hidden quality they might have. Two well-dressed gentlemen, for example, were checking out a plastic sphere. Their conversation went like this:

> *(One fellow, picking the item up)* *"Wow, look at this, Harry!"*
>
> *"What is it?"*
>
> *"I don't know, but it's heavy and it feels good."*
>
> *The other man, now suitably enthused with the find, said, "Well, it's only eighty-eight cents—let's get it!"*

Most of us would like to think we'd never be this dumb about acquisition, and that maybe we would exercise admirable prudence in the "under a dollar" stores. But once we are immersed in the ambience of a shopping mall or store of any kind, even the tiniest temptation can trigger a full-scale inclination to shoot the works. We settle on, "Well, it's only $29.95 . . . let's get it."

Am I telling you to resist the temptation of accumulation? Nope. I'm telling you to *avoid* the temptation. None of us are as good at resisting as we imagine we are. You don't have to be an expert at refusing offers if you aren't present when the offer is made.

Amazing, how many ads and catalogs we don't need to read once we savor the pleasures of being clutter-free.

Remember the Difference Between Wants and Needs

We've all been told about the difference between wants and needs, but most of us still don't have this quite sorted out yet.

By instinct, we want it all, and there are many brilliant financiers and marketers who work day and night to find a way to make it possible for us to obtain it all. Remember the difference between wants and needs, and beware of the steady move from wants . . . to needs . . . to deeds!

Think: Why Are You Buying This?

The following are the boiled-down basic reasons we accumulate clutter in our homes and storage areas. We usually buy something because:

- We want to show it off (flaunt it)
- We intend to use it (but do we?)
- We're going to stash it away
- We're "addicted" (couldn't say no)
- "It's an investment" (lots of wishful thinking here)
- We were bored

We accumulate a lot of our clutter just for something to do. We wander around collecting stuff and then looking for a place to store it or a sentence to explain why we have it. The next time you're tempted to buy something, stop long enough to figure out why you want it.

> Don't ever underestimate the combination of idleness, exposure, and convenience as an accelerator of accumulation and "I wonder why I bought this?"

Consider Obsolescence

Always consider the obsolescence potential of anything you're considering taking on or making part of your life. What doesn't last and is no longer loved will always put weight on you in some way.

As a friend pointed out to me wistfully one day, "Ah yes, I just had to have one of those big satellite dishes [$5,000 when they first came out!]. I feed the cattle hay out of it now."

New May Be Better . . . But Is It Necessary?

One big source of clutter is always having to have new and better when the old is working fine. Every salesperson's aim is to make us dissatisfied with "the old one." But out of date doesn't mean out of service. Not long ago, I dug out my nearly fifty-year-old Nikon F2, blew off the dust, loaded it up with film, put in a new battery, and shot some pictures at a church picnic. The prints were so clear people peered at them in amazement, and it took all of 1/8 of a second to focus by hand each time. I look around and see camera waste on every side, a shelf or drawer full of automated, do-it-all-for-you models, for just one person. And very few pictures are actually being taken.

In my shop, too, I have tools that are just as fast as the newer automated ones, that don't break down, and that don't need batteries or electric cords. Many of these are thirty and forty years old and older. Why should I be in such a rush to "upgrade"?

High-tech medical gear and some computer and phone equipment might merit immediate update, but don't be too quick to abandon those old manual models. Many modern machines are so complicated and automatic that after a while, we often just don't use them. It's not worth the mental strain to read and digest the 110-page booklet that comes with them and figure out how to use all the options.

Why are we always wanting more and better when we aren't using the things we already have?

The urge to own the newest and best and latest technology creates a lot of clutter and credit card debt. People constantly ask me how I can get along without a cell phone. Though I own and manage companies in several states, and have family, community, and church matters to tend to all over, I haven't felt the need for a cell phone yet. Nor do I really want to be interrupted by one everywhere, or distracted by one while driving. All of my managers have them, and what I mostly see (while I'm riding with them) is them calling spouses on their way home to tell them what time they will be home. This is something they could do from the office more cheaply and courteously. My point here is not that I am against cell phones—in some businesses and circumstances they are a real asset, or even essential. But having a cell phone when you don't really need one is just another tool to pay for, hunt for, tend to, and guard—all in all, making life harder, not easier, to live.

Or consider that famous garage tool so many hobbyists aspire to: the Shopsmith, a machine capable of performing the tasks of a dozen different power tools. Yet the majority of these amazing mutants are used mainly as simple table saws in the end. They are much more costly than a table saw, and it's harder to isolate a problem when they need fixing.

Computers, likewise, can do an unbelievable number of things—it's true. However, many computer owners are at the point of panic over this. They don't want, need, use, or understand all of the extras their machines are packed with. The average person probably uses only about 15 percent of the features and capacities of all of their computer programs and hardware. A few aficionados demand ever more options and bells and whistles, while the average person helps pay for it all but uses only a few. She could probably get along just as well with the "older" version of software and hardware she already has. This is another case when new may not be necessary.

Use what you have. "Getting by" and "making do" were once not just the standard, but something to be admired.

People talk constantly about getting back to the basics, even as they are gearing up to get more, bigger, better, and faster—behavior that only takes them ever farther from the basics.

Beware of Gadgets

I've made many in-person appearances at home shows, those garden or home remodeling shows held every spring and fall at huge arenas or convention centers. The aisles are lined with hundreds or even thousands of booths, merchants giving shows and demonstrations on everything imaginable—from hot tubs to salad makers, ginseng to knife sets. On every side is someone showing and selling a magic tool or miracle formula, while thousands of people shuffle by, taking it all in.

It never ceases to amaze me that the biggest crowds always seem to be gathered at the booths with the most questionable products. People watch and believe the pitchman, who saw the product for the first time himself three hours ago. Then they clamor to lay down a chunk of cash for a handy-dandy, rinky-dinky thing they'll never use or that won't work once they get it home. The glamour and glitter of gadgets pulls people out of good sense and propels them to purchase, pack home, piddle with, and then stick the gadget someplace to crowd the cabinet or rattle around in a drawer. Be warned when your heart starts warming toward some new gadget. Get solid tools, not gadgets.

Don't Buy Things You Can't Use

This is a day of "owned but not used." I was the major employer in Sun Valley, Idaho, a ski resort town, for six years. During the course of this, I did a lot of maintenance and repair work in and around nice homes. Sun Valley had become a place where movie stars and other rich people came and overpaid for property and put up huge homes worth millions of dollars. The elegance of these homes was a topic of conversation for every tradesperson working in them. Many of these homes were built long distance—the owners never showed up during the process, and the builders and workers just received calls and messages from the owners about things to be done. Then, after the house was finished, it sat vacant most of the time because the owner was too busy or far away to use it much. These edifices were mostly good for magazine articles on them, so that all of us with ordinary little homes could drool over them. This giant and expensive piece of property was of little value to the owner—just something to plan, to build, to protect, to maintain, and to pay for forever.

"I have three fly rods and I haven't fished for five years. Maybe I'll buy another one, and that will compensate for not going fishing as much." (Junker's logic)

We all do this on a smaller scale. We may criticize the big spenders, but a lot of rash spending of even small amounts equals the same outcome. Don't buy things, large or small, that you can't or won't use.

Forget "SALE"

If you want to see motivation for acquiring more, even for those with "too much," just remove the "for" from a "for sale" sign. Almost everything is for sale, but used alone, "SALE" becomes the most powerful, seductive word in our language. Even the best defenses are breached when there is wind of a real sale. You can get another of something you have and don't use, and you can get it cheaper than the first one. (Then we buy it on our credit cards, where the interest often pushes the cost higher than the presale price ever was.) "Wholesale" and "factory outlet" likewise numb our noodles, and price clubs and co-ops have a way of convincing us that because it costs a little less, we have a right—a need—to claim it!

A husband, for example, bought his wife a wholesale club card and went in to look the store over. He ended up carrying three shopping carts of stuff out. Need wasn't the decision factor; it was just that the deals were too great—you could get two for one, even if you really didn't need the one. (My wife admits she has twelve pairs of two-for-one shoes she hasn't worn once yet.) Another woman, whose children are all grown now, bought one gallon of hot-dog relish because the price was just too low to pass up. That big jug is still jamming her refrigerator, and she's still passing out free jars of relish to everyone she knows.

The word "sale" is bad enough, now just add the word "season" and even the firmest of us will fold—winter, spring, summer, and fall sales give us permission to pile up the place.

> "The only difference between a yard sale and a trash pickup is how close to the road the stuff is placed."

"Trouble" sales really make us buy, too, because when others are in a forced situation, we just know they are bottom-dollar desperate. Lost-our-lease sales, out-of-business sales, clearance sales, fire sales, inventory sales, and moving sales will move us to action. Even if we have no money or space to put anything more, we'll be there at 6:00 A.M. Stick a number in front of "sale," too, and watch out! Thirty percent, 40 percent, or 50 percent off will mesmerize us into taking in a glut. A famous person's name will work this magic, too—Washington, Lincoln, Columbus, even the Easter bunny linked up with "sale" means one more chance to get the good deals. "Yard sale" is a cheap shot, but watch a crooked cardboard sign with these words scribbled on it pull in the passers-buyer!

The Word "SAVE"—A Real Seducer

"Save," too, is a real seducer, and a prime example is long-distance calling. As competition in the industry has increased, it's driven prices down, which is one reason for all those sales calls we get from MCI, Sprint, AT&T, and all the rest of the pack, asking us to sign up for their latest system because we will "save so much."

With all of these savings, are our phone bills lower? No way. Home phone bills, which once were ten or twenty dollars, are now into the hundreds. Why? Because calls are now so "cheap" that we are doubling and tripling our phone use. We think that with each call we are saving, so the more calls we make, the more we save. . . . That's pretty poor logic, and millions now have stunning long distance and cellular phone costs to prove it. By the end of the month, we've spent $200 instead of the $50 we would have spent when the prices were so high.

"Sale" and "save" are entirely immaterial to something we don't need, something that isn't necessary in our life. Our crew traveled down to El Paso, Texas, once, for example, to give a workshop on cleaning up your place and possessions. We gave our presentation to an enthusiastic crowd, leaving them committed to cutting down clutter and cleaning time. I had one last speech to give alone, which left the rest of my crew with some free time to do whatever they wanted. There was not a drop of doubt or delay—in an instant, they were headed across the border to Mexico, only three miles away.

"What are you going to do there?" I asked.

"Buy stuff," was the answer.

"Such as what?" I questioned. (They'd all been complaining about their overloaded homes on the drive down.)

"Well, nothing we can think of right this minute, but . . . "

"But what?"

"Things are so cheap there, Don! Leather wallets, for instance, are only about a quarter of the price they are here in the States."

"But you have at least a dozen good wallets already."

"You just don't understand—they are so inexpensive. . . . "

True, I just don't understand!

How many of us have extra wallets around, and haven't been across a border yet?

Forget "Deals"

When you hear someone say that a deal was "a steal," you've heard a great truth. Most deals steal your time, money, emotion, wits, and space. One woman, who started collecting back in 1960, now has over 1,000 cookbooks. She said her entire collection started from a brochure on a cookbook club addressed to "Resident," wherein for just one dollar you could get three books. She picked the largest, on the assumption that they would tell her the most, and you know the rest now.

> "Since I dejunked, I've saved all that time I used to spend every day scanning ads and newspapers for deals. Junk-free is the best deal I ever made or got."

A while ago, a young couple I know were excited about a coming trip to Las Vegas. I asked them why they were going there, as I knew they didn't gamble, weren't drinkers, and weren't even particularly entertainment oriented. Plus, they had a little family and both worked, so they would have to be away from their children and their jobs for a few days. Their reason for going?

"It was so cheap! We got air fare, a rental car, and two nights in a motel for $98."

"All because it is a deal," I noted.

"More than a deal," they said. "Even a bargain trip to Las Vegas normally costs about $400, so we are saving $300, and we just couldn't pass that up."

Amazing. They were willing to spend several days away from home, wandering through a bunch of noise and lights, doing things they didn't particularly enjoy, mainly because it was a bargain.

> "At our rummage sale, we finally marked a rickety old desk down from $20 to $1. The buyer was so enthused and tickled with his 'bargain,' that he gouged his $30,000 Trans Am trying to shove that worthless, falling-apart old thing into the trunk."

"Go" Doesn't Have to Mean "Get"

Bringing home to a spouse, child, or coworker a gift from a trip can indeed be a nice little addition to the quality of life. But things aren't like they used to be. Not long ago, only a few traveled, and only once in a while. Now most of us are mobile, and some of us take ten or more trips in a single month! Our base of relationships has broadened, too. As time passes, our family and circle of friends grows bigger, and there are more people who work with, for, and around us. All of which triples, if not quadruples, the number of people eagerly awaiting gifts when you get back.

For years I worked to keep up the pace of procuring things worth giving as gifts to family and friends when I returned. It threatened to become the central focus of my trips. I had to plan my purchases before a trip, and make them on the way there and while there (sometimes missing meetings to do it). Then I had to cushion breakables and find a way to keep perishables cool, to carry awkward things, and to protect all the packages on the way home. After all this effort, much of the time, the recipients either already had what I got them or had no place to put it. So a harmless little thing became much and then too much. Now that I limit my travel gifts, I've noticed neither hostility nor longing glances at my suitcases when I return. Instead I see a marked increase in my own productivity in my travels, which ultimately blesses everyone more than any number of trashy trinkets lugged home could.

"Go" doesn't have to mean "get," although we seem to have been taught that somehow. On the cover of a senior citizens' magazine once, for example, I noticed a big feature article titled "Going Places." I figured this would be about making trips or excursions that would expand our talents and outlook, and maybe our circle of friends and acquaintances . . . until I read the fine print under the title: "Cruising, food, wine, and bargains. . . . " Going places this way won't do anything to declutter our golden years.

In our effort to get away from it all, we have the tendency to take it all with us. In tourist or convention towns, the streets are lined with gift shops—the exact sort of thing that most people have traveled to get away from. But there they are, right in the Mecca of "too much," and soon they are walking out with armloads of stuff they didn't want or need, and that they don't know what to do with or where to store.

A couple I know were traveling on a tour boat through some of the most beautiful land in Alaska. They had five hours of shore leave and used it all walking the streets, where there was nothing but souvenir shops. A focus on "getting something" in life often takes too much time and attention away from "becoming something" personally. We seem to think of acquiring in terms of hardware, rather than the emotions we might experience just letting something be absorbed into our being—a feeling, a song, a view, an insight. Instead, we seem to opt for a chunk of wood, plastic, or metal or a piece of cloth with a saying on it. Our relentless pursuit of "too much" blocks out many of the finer things of life.

Nothing is Duty-Free

Getting ready to board a flight one day, I noticed passengers loaded down with much more than travel luggage—they had stuff sticking out of every conceivable style of bag and bundle. The source of this seemed to be the duty-free shop and its enticing array of liquors, tobacco, perfumes, jewelry, and gifts.

That took nerve, calling this stuff "duty-free." Nothing is duty-free. If it adds even an extra ounce of weight, you'll be paying that duty tax in installments for years thereafter.

Forget "FREE"

At a home show once, a 200-foot-long line filed past the booth where I was doing vacuum demonstrations. I asked the people in it, "What line is this?"

They answered, "I don't know, but whatever they are offering, I want one!"

Once, during the taping of a TV program I was to appear on, to get the studio audience warmed up, the host yelled, "How many of you would like to get some free stuff?" Enthusiastic cheers, shrieks, and yells ensued, though no one in that audience had a clue as to what was to be given away. But it was *free*. The evaluation of bad or good, needed or not needed, is totally blotted out by "free."

In the final stages of planning and designing our low-maintenance home on Kauai, for example, my wife and I decided to go to the annual home-and-garden show in Honolulu. So we called to get information and tickets to the event itself and the plane trip to it. There was (of course) a "deal" that included a free rental car with the flight. My wife excitedly reported this bonus to me. "But we don't need a car," I told her.

"It won't cost us one cent more," she said. "We've got to take it!"

Yes, the car was free, but . . . I explained the costs to her: "After we arrive in Honolulu, we can walk the fifty feet from the Aloha Airlines gate to catch a fast city bus for $1, which will take us right to the front steps of the exhibition center. Then just $1 for the return trip, no stress, and we can sit back and enjoy all the sights on the way. That 'free' car is going to take one hour to check out and check in, insurance and gas will be $30 or more, parking at the convention center will take twenty minutes and cost $5, and then finding maps and driving in the congested downtown of an unfamiliar city isn't exactly my idea of a day off." The free car was a wonderful example of how "free" can end up costing us wasted time, money, and emotion. Most free things end up kicking around the house or cluttering up a storage area somewhere.

"My friend got a free car through an ad in the paper. It had been in a front-end collision and had lots of body rust. It also needed a new radiator, a new alternator, and I don't know what else. I'd love to see how much she spent in insurance, title transfer, and repairs on this 'free' car."

Don't Take Things Just Because They're There

Why do we do it? Most of us do: We get a voucher, a per diem allowance, or a budget for food, for example—such as when we're on a business trip or our flight is delayed—and we force ourselves to use it all up. Often we don't need it, we aren't hungry, but it is ours; we have a coupon for it or it's being served, so we strain to use it all. There seems to be some stigma about leaving anything for someone else, or just skipping the "free lunch." I've watched super-intelligent and ignorant people alike inflict stress and indigestion on themselves as they try to use all of a voucher to "get their money's worth."

We'll always take samples of food, yardsticks, pens, free newspapers or magazines, stickers, ball caps, or key chains. It's as if availability were the question, and not what is needed or right for us.

"I grew up with a mother whose favorite sayings were:

1. 'That's a perfectly good _____.' (This was usually said while viewing someone else's trash, and yes, we always snatched up the item in question.)

2. 'Stop the car!!!' (This was to pick up other people's trash, or for any garage sale anywhere.)
3. 'Someone could use that.' (It usually wasn't us.)"

Forget "My Share"

Ever really think about what "your share" means? Share is seldom evaluated in terms of what will actually benefit us, only as to whether or not we got an equal portion of a commodity at hand. A "right" to something doesn't necessarily mean we need, deserve, or have to have it. Look how slow we are to claim our share of debt or blame, and how demanding we can be when it comes to a piece of cake, an allotment, an inheritance, or a handout. Going for a share just because it is there invests you in "Too Much, Incorporated."

Hold Down the Holidays

One February, I looked at the upcoming and ever-expanding Valentine season and realized I was in an "all or nothing" valentine-sending situation. I decided on the nothing, and so didn't give one single valentine, not even to my wife, who said, "Hooray, we saved money, clutter, and time that could be better spent."

Don't get me wrong—I've long been a fan of the spirit of the day. In grade school, Valentine's Day was the sensation of the year in some boring classes and drab buildings. Valentines were a wonderful experience clear through the eighth grade.

My decision to have a "heartless" February 14 was reinforced when my wife and I (though we were 2,500 miles apart) both went to different local stores and saw several *aisles* full of Valentine's Day stuff. Families were buying $30 and $40 worth of red trash, candy they didn't need, plus plaques, pillows, stuffed animals, and other trinkets—most of which would be ignored within hours of receipt by whomever received them. Today, there isn't just one sweetheart, a mother, and maybe a favorite aunt to consider. It would be a formidable undertaking to include in your Valentine remembrances everyone that the card aisles and catalogs would have you include . . . enough to make you heartsick!

We have a similar problem with Halloween, and also Easter. Once you get on the holiday hayride, it will take you for a ride—doing the steering, stopping, and loading for you, all at your expense.

Don't be afraid to trim back the holidays to fit your own situation, means, taste, or feelings. You'll have less stress, less clutter, and you'll enjoy even more the days you do celebrate.

Make Your Path Public

We don't acquire all of our excess intentionally—some of it comes in the form of gifts, awards, inheritance, handouts, junk mail, or other "freebies." We didn't seek it out, but somehow we ended up housing it.

One thing that will help here is to make your standards and policies about junk and clutter clear to everyone . . . everywhere. Then, others will stop giving you, sending you, or even offering you anything of questionable worth. Shed your unwanted stuff publicly and others will get the idea fast. Before you toss some silly or ugly piece of clutter, tell the world that you didn't want it and haven't got space for anything like it. Have no clutter around you, and people will avoid filling your space. As soon as they get the message that you aren't messing around and that managing stuff isn't your favorite pastime, they will lay off laying it on you.

You'll know you've gotten the message across when people start complaining, "Boy, are you hard to buy for." What a compliment it is when people are afraid to give you anything that might fall under the category of "junk." You'll have less unsolicited clutter, and the quality of the gifts you do get will improve dramatically.

Look at Your Lifestyle

Sometime—preferably this weekend—stop and look at your lifestyle. Maybe it is your way of living that is causing the result you aren't pleased with. Long-established habits such as shopping for entertainment, fad following, hobby hopping, or overkill of any kind may be encouraging that frightening flow of clutter to your car, mailbox, and closets.

Live Lean

My father was a master manager, and the older I get, the more I search back into the memories of the years we worked together. I think about the ways he managed to be so productive in his life, for the benefit of not only our whole ranching operation but every one of us in the family.

One of these ways was his habit of living lean. We lived well—better than kings—but lean. Nothing ever seemed crowded, excessive, overdone. At Fourth of July picnics or Thanksgiving or Christmas feasts where there was more food than we can comprehend now, Dad always ate one plateful. Leaving the table a little hungry, rather than "overstuffed," always gives you an edge for staying healthy and active. People who live it up are usually rewarded by having to live it down. Dad's theory was "live lighter, live better," an opposite philosophy from the majority of marketing and merchandising messages.

Don't Be Afraid to Go Without

Fortunately, I come from people who had the foresight to record their lives in journals, and generations later these were collected into a family history book. It's fascinating to read about my forebears boating from Europe, establishing colonies in the New World, and crossing the plains. But it's even more amazing to read about what and how well they endured, battling snowstorms and droughts, wild animals, hunger, injury, illness, and sudden violent death. Hardships only seemed to strengthen their family closeness and ideals. Loyalty, love, and simple things provided a savor we seem to be searching for earnestly now but cannot find.

These histories offer clear evidence that a crisp, rewarding life can indeed be lived without a sports car, fancy clothes, lavish jewelry, big houses and yards, portfolios of investments, and perks of all kinds.

If you talk to the people today who had to "go without" at some time in life, most of their comments on this are positive. People see it as a good and valuable experience, a time of closeness and building and learning. Even those who have experienced some real struggles often say that living with less and going without was the best time of their lives, in retrospect. They did more, felt more, and grew and developed as people more—it was a time of real closeness to family and nature. Then we get well heeled enough to go anyplace or do or own anything and life begins to close in on us.

> How many of the beautifully printed pages of our best-known magazines are devoted to how to get and own every new, automatic, overdesigned this and that; exotic, expensive food, clothes, and destinations; and accessories, movie stars, glamour, and cosmetics?

Coping with Those Cluttered Choices

Our grandparents and great-grandparents really had limited choices and opportunities. There were only a few things available to wear, buy, travel in, read, or entertain yourself or others with. So, considering the alternatives and making choices and judgments was relatively simple. Sometimes they didn't even have a choice!

Our parents had a new world of more products, machines, and services than ever before, and much more widespread ways of making the availability of all this known to them. And look at you and me and everyone today—as noted earlier, we have an endless galaxy of opportunities. We have much more money, greater access to everything, a seemingly unlimited World Wide Web of information, and no end to the products and brands to buy and places to go. With the aid of extended payment plans and credit cards, we can own or have almost anything we want, do anything we want, go anywhere we please. All of us have more to choose from than kings did a few hundred years ago. So, understandably, we are getting bogged down—if not stuck—in the consideration and selection process.

There is so much, even in the average store, we actually have to stop life to consider the options before we can proceed with whatever we're about. We could easily spend a month of our lives reading labels in the cereal aisle of the supermarket alone.

This is not to say that all the opportunities available these days are bad, because they aren't. Many of them are blessings, but the limiting factor here is that we can't want and have it all (Lord knows we're trying)—most of us can't afford it and we haven't the room to retain it. Just think for a minute about how much you have on hold or under consideration; how much you want, are waiting for, or are fully or halfheartedly pursuing. It might be magnificent stuff, but it soon becomes just more pounds of burden.

Another Answer—Direction!

There is a big benefit in doing "media" (appearing on TV and radio and in newspapers) besides the publicity. Those reporters, hosts, and commentators are always pushing and hounding you for a short succinct, bottom-line answer to the problems at hand, and they ask questions such as "Why do people become junkers, Don?"

Over the years, from thousands of voluntary contributors and confessed clutterers, I've built up quite a list of why's. Like, "It was a gift," sentiment, vanity, "I was raised during the Depression," heredity, the environment, insecurity, etc. There are pages of reasons. When I squeeze these people like the media squeeze me for a one-word or one-sentence summary, it generally boils down to . . . indecision. We just can't decide what, when, and where, so we take everything that is there.

That's the bottom line—so what is the *cause* of that indecision? Here lies what I believe is the real core of life's clutter: *lack of direction*! It's that simple. When you know where you are going, you know what to carry. Most of the overloaded can't tell you what they really want in life. Direction is somewhat of a mystery to them. I'm meeting more people than ever these days who give me a blank look when I ask, "What are your life goals, where are you going, what are you doing this for?" They don't know, so they try to cover all the bases and provide for every possibility. Notice that people who really know what they are doing and why—their life purpose—seem to carry a minimum of extras. People who are a little confused about what they want and where they are headed take as much as they can carry, just in case . . . (they might need it someday).

You need direction before you can cut down the "too much" traffic in your life. Needs are easy to see and decisions almost make themselves once you've established a clear direction. All of us have the strength and smarts for the "what" and "how" to get rid of clutter once we see what we really need to get where we want to go. Once you map out your intended journey, you'll know what to pack.

So sit down after you've dejunked your things this weekend and spend one of the most important hours of your life deciding, determining, or simply articulating your goals. Write out what you really want to do in the next year, decade, or the rest of your life. Staying junk-free will be much easier afterward.

Now What About . . . Our Environmental Excesses?

In recent years, we've listened to and read the warnings of all kinds of experts, advising that the earth's natural systems are being threatened from all directions. By what? We already know the answer—too much!

What are some of these environmental issues?

- Air pollution and global warming (the air we need to breathe and the ozone layer we need to protect us)
- Water pollution (which affects the water we drink and like to play in)
- Litter and clutter
- Household waste
- Hazardous waste
- Deforestation and loss of wetlands (including loss of habitat for wild animals and birds)
- Land erosion (loss of the topsoil we need to grow our food)
- Mineral/oil depletion

True, we do have to live. However, if you review this list thoughtfully, you'll see that the overload here is not from what we need or use to live, but from too much. We (ourselves and our country as a whole) could cut all of these down by as much as 50 percent if we only controlled what we use, what we waste, how we eat, and how we treat things.

We are approaching this problem like we do other problems—we continue to heap it on, and then after a while, we complain and go for the girdle cure. And so our solution here is to make laws and regulations that only organize and regulate the excess, rarely actually reducing it.

For years now, for example, panic-stricken "do-gooders" have been telling us that, before long, we are going to bury ourselves in our own trash. They are right—we are! Like most of you, I grew up counting on the city, the county, or a commercial garbage hauler to pick up all those "leftovers" and make them disappear. And the taxes and charges for this weren't too bad. Now those fees are going up, and we hear everywhere about how there is too much waste and trash, and there's not enough room for it all. Barges are circling harbors searching for a new dumping place. And it's not just a big-city problem. I live in Idaho, where we have more than forty acres per person. But I'm also in the profession of cleaning buildings and handling the fallout from them, and I, too, see what is happening. There is indeed too much trash, and we (if not you and me, then our grandchildren or great-grandchildren and their loved ones) are going to be buried by it.

The fact that we ignore this will never make it go away. The earth's obesity problem isn't a social one as we are told; it is an individual problem—government, cities, counties, or clubs can't control it. Consider the "Adopt a Highway" program. The more do-gooders police up those beer and soda cans, the more litter there is. People are tossing more than ever, and we are cleaning up behind them, only reinforcing bad environmental behavior. The junk and clutter is still there; we are just wasting good gas and risking lives policing it. It is self-policing, not policing, that will save the earth. I may never manage to distribute my extra food to a foreign country, but I can avoid waste, luxury, and excess that will ultimately affect the welfare of the entire world. If enough of us did this, it would make a big difference.

"Too much" is an action demand, and that action needs to be initiated not by any group, club, or government agency, but by each and every one of us as individuals.

To keep the weight off Mother Nature, we all need to live providently:

1. Waste less
2. Buy less
3. Eat less
4. Use, do not abuse, facilities
5. Clean up our own messes
6. Travel less and stay home more
7. Un-cycle (stop adding things to the system), and then worry about recycling
8. Stop smoking (not just ourselves, but our cars and our buildings)
9. Deglamorize ourselves, our homes, our vehicles, and our habits

This will do more than all the marches, donations, legislation, campaigns, and pledges.

Embrace a new word, "minimalism," to balance out wastefulness and materialism.

The Ten Commandments of Keeping Free

1. Honor all good habits that cost and clutter less.
2. Thou shalt not "shop." Just purchase the necessities.
3. Make thy path public. Announce your weightless state so people won't fill your mind, mouth, or living room shelves with stuff.
4. Thou shalt not commit credit card escalation.

5. Thou shalt not covet "sale" merchandise.

6. Ban junk bunkers (furnishings, accessories, or structures that do nothing but hold and encourage junk).

7. Do not honor gray areas. It is either Yes you need it or No you don't. Thou shalt not say "maybe," permitting questionable objects to occupy middle ground.

8. Thou shalt not get the shakes when you have extra room, space, or savings.

9. Hang around with the trim and uncluttered, and you won't have hang-ups or clutter hangovers.

10. Thou shalt reflect daily upon how much more efficient, better off, and better liked you are when you're clutter free!

Chapter 9

Too Wonderful for Words!

A doctor, who had been a young Air Force commander in World War II, gave me an example of unloading I never forgot. He said, "Getting off the ground in England with the tons and tons of weight in a bomber was almost touch and go. The plane struggled to gain altitude, and it flew heavy. As soon as we crossed over into enemy territory, the anti-aircraft fire and flack were intense. We had all those explosives on board, and bullets and shells were hitting and exploding all around us and often zipping through the fuselage and cockpit. But we had to wait until we reached the target area before we could release our deadly cargo.

"When the bomb bay doors finally opened and the bombs dropped in plummeting clusters to the munitions factories below, the crew breathed a collective sigh of relief. And the plane lunged upward like a roller coaster, almost uncontrollably, with all that weight gone! No matter how prepared we were for this de-weighting, it was always an amazing sensation."

I lived that intense and unforgettable experience with him as he described it, and thought of how in my own life, when I finally release problems, how my energy and spirit lunge and soar upward, too . . . being lighter is its own reward.

On a large network radio show once, I asked people to call in and confess to the biggest pieces of clutter they wanted— but just hadn't managed—to get rid of. We offered a prize for the worst junk, and there were some lulus. The winner was a woman who had a school bus in the backyard—old and rusty, wheels and motor gone, set up on blocks and used for storage.

About a year later, she phoned in during another call-in show to tell me she finally had it hauled away. I asked her what kind of reward she got, from the neighbors or otherwise, and she offered a classic statement: "No other reward was necessary—when it was gone, I had my view back." That's a pretty profound reward for dejunking, or in this case losing 20,000 pounds of clutter in one day!

As you declutter, you, like the young flyers, will be so surprised. It will be so much better than you anticipated. As you divest yourself of excess, you will discover an unheralded truth of life: less is more, and it brings with it beautiful words such as . . . "trim," "lean," "in proportion," "free," "peaceful."

There are hundreds of rewards for removal of the "too much." Here's a reminder about the big three:

1. You'll have more room. In your rooms, your closets, your drawers, and your imagination, and on your agenda. Room is a wonderful reward—room to breathe, to think, to put out and place nicely the precious things you've been saving "until later." Room means less stumbling over things and hunting through them, and less explaining, to yourself and others, about the crowded condition of your life.

2. You'll have more time for the things you really care about. When you get rid of the garbage, you can do more of the good things.
3. You'll feel better, and be treated better by everyone!

Real-Life Testimonies from Born-Again Former Junkers

"I can't believe how flexible and free I feel without clutter!"

"I now go places and enjoy instead of buying stuff with my time."

"Success, oh sweet success. It took me just fifteen minutes to clear the entire room for the tile installer. Before dejunking my life, it would have taken me one solid week. Ah, the junkless life, I love it!"

"I love my clean and spacious house now. I love knowing where things are! I LOVE NOT BEING A JOKE AND A MESS!"

"Psychologically, I am someone else now. I have time to go outside with my kids and to play on the floor with them."

"How do I feel now that I've decluttered? How have I most benefited from the process? I've lost weight, dumped fears, discarded illusions, chucked insecurities, obtained confidences, secured a brighter future, increased my productivity, improved the quality of my life, and sent the 'bigger, better, and more is better yet' philosophy packing."

"There is just something eloquent about being uncluttered."

"The biggest benefit I got from dejunking is that now I know what I have and don't have, and exactly where everything is. Three months ago I could never find a pair of scissors when I needed them."

"The biggest surprise is not so much the freedom I feel after dejunking, but the horror I feel when I walk into others' homes and see how shackled they are by their junk. It makes me want to shake them and make them realize what their junk is doing to them."

"Thanks again for being one of the biggest influences in my whole life!! I know you have helped so many people who, like me, had kept wondering how to manage all this stuff. Your wonderful answer, at least it worked for me, was: GET RID OF IT!"

"God bless you for your work in throwing us clutterholics a lifeline."

"You have changed my life!"

"I have a lot less to clean. I can see all the way under my bed. I can walk freely through my room without following a path. I am a much happier person to be around because I have a lot less on my mind. I don't worry about whether or not I lock my door."

"You've even affected my eating habits. I have a lot less physical, emotional, and mental baggage now. My friends can sense the difference in me. I've started cleaning up my habits of cursing and eating junk food. I have more self-esteem and a better self-image. You've done more for me in three weeks of reading your books than counselors have done in ten years of weekly therapy."

The Big Bonus of the Makeover Weekend

The excess that is weighing us down, as we well know, is more than old shoes, broken furniture, and heavy boxes of old magazines. These are the tangible excesses. The real toughies to toss are the harmful habits. We know what these are—we could all make a long list of the nasty little things we do, readily admitting that they are harmful to our health, our friends, and our conscience. But being told to drop the habits—"Don't get mad anymore!" "Quit coming late!" "Stop drinking all that soda!" "Drive safely!" "Don't swear!"—is never going to provide the willpower, commitment, or discipline to enable us to reform. These intangible excesses (much to our frustration) have a way of really hanging on until we outgrow or outlive them. Many people, sad to say, never savor the freedom of conquering them.

Here is the bonus of the makeover weekend, and any like weekends that follow. Removing tangible junk and clutter is ten times easier than shedding those emotional intangibles. So, first, do what you have to do to rid yourself of all the old treasures that have turned to trash. Read *Clutter's Last Stand, 2nd Edition* (or read it again, if you've already read it), if you want any more information about the principles and pro-cedures involved. And here is my promise: As those tangible items go out of your life and finally leave some room, a quiet confidence will seep into your soul and testify to you that you don't need "stuff" to be happy.

When you are rid of all that weight you used to deal with daily around your place, you will at last have the self-esteem you've been seeking for so long and in so many ways. Plus, you'll also experience a stream of other related virtues such as efficiency, strength, endurance, and a sense of confidence and security. And the best part: With the shedding of this clutter, there will often be an automatic shedding of mental weights like depression and grudges, and the aura of lean will even influence the old diet department. It all flows together and is a surefire formula for finding freedom from any weight. The biggest reward of all here is the carryover from the pat-tern you'll establish—a formula for further personal growth, freedom, and happiness.

The Real Bottom Line of Dejunking

But what is the real bottom line of dejunking, cleaning up your life, and taking charge of what and who you are, essen-tially gaining freedom from your burdens? Now you have the capacity to serve others! That is what you are doing all this for—so that you are squared away enough to help and take care of those in need. Service is the only way humans are ever satisfied. Having, eating, sports, sex, or travel—all these bring a little rush to our lives, but never the blessing we need to be truly happy.

As one reformed junkaholic put it, "I love people and this earth and I want to make a difference." This is the greatest of all rewards, helping others, the more the merrier!

What type of service you might want to pursue is another book and another story, but the answer is deep inside you. You already know what and why to give of yourself. And the minute you aren't fighting your own battles of what is in, on, and around you, you will have a clearer vision of the needs of others—plus the time, energy, and desire to help. As the saying goes, "Life doesn't get any better than this!"

A Personal Code That Works for Me

Here is a personal code that has really worked for me to help prevent all that clutter from creeping back in. I call it "Living Providently"—the big ten.

1. Keep yourself and your place, space, and possessions clean and orderly—uncluttered with no excess.
2. Keep yourself in top physical and emotional condition.
3. Spend less—in accord with your financial capacity and need, not what the neighbors have or what the networks or the Internet have to offer.
4. Think of your vehicle as a safe, economical mode of transportation—not a matter of ego or status.
5. Work hard—be eagerly engaged in a good cause.
6. Stay home more. Don't waste your real estate. Make home your life center, not the malls, shops, cafes, and stadiums.
7. Take real advantage of what you have before expanding or getting more.
8. Know the difference between a standard of living and a standard of luxury.
9. Create minimum waste—to help save your personal and our public environment.
10. Take care of those in need and ease others' burdens when you can. Save souls instead of stuff.

The Last Excuse Eliminated!

And now the last excuse for not decluttering defused. Of all of the comments people make after their makeover weekends, which of the following would you guess is the most common?

1. "I'm free at last!" Nope.
2. "Wow, I have more room now." Nope.
3. "Gads! I made a heap of money on that old saved stuff." Nope.
4. "I can't believe I didn't do this sooner!" Nope.
5. "I've totally quit mall cruising and going to garage sales." Nope.
6. "My cars are all parked inside for the first time in twenty years!" Nope.
7. "My family and friends all admire me now." Nope.

All of the above are, in fact, frequent testimonies, but the single most common remark is, *"I can't believe it, Don—I haven't missed any of it!"* Now there is the best reason not to procrastinate our escape from the excess that is now ripping us off. Great, huh?

Acknowledgments

First, a heartfelt thank-you to you, my readers and audiences. I'd never be able to keep on writing worthwhile books about dejunking without your help. The clutter problems and solutions you write and e-mail me about, and tell me about in person, keep giving me new and fresh insights and real-life examples that would stimulate any writer.

Thanks also to Craig LaGory, whose illustration and design made the first edition of this book a winner. And to Hazel Cotton, Tricia Hoffman, Sandra Phillips, Stefanye Ghormley, and my other clutter scouts and "constant clippers."

Finally, this book and my other books on the subject would never be what they are without my editor and longtime clutter collaborator, Carol Cartaino. Yes, she's still the head packrat (I think she has nine buildings full of junk now!).

Index

About the Author

DON ASLETT, America's #1 Cleaning and Decluttering Expert, has been a professional cleaner for more than fifty years. He has written more than thirty books, many of them bestsellers, including *Clutter's Last Stand*, *For Packrats Only*, *Clutter Free! Finally and Forever*, and perhaps his best known, *Is There Life After Housework?*

Don is the founder and guru of the "dejunking" movement, and this is now his fifth book on the subject, one of the most pressing problems of the modern world. He is 110 percent convinced that much of what we find unsatisfactory and unsettling in our lives can be removed by a simple three-word solution: *"Dejunk your life."* This book, and all of his others, is meant to persuade and help readers do just that.

Don (who still thinks working fourteen hours a day is pure enjoyment) is the chairman of the board of Varsity Contractors, a national facility services (cleaning and maintenance) company; a noted and popular speaker; and a regular guest on radio and TV. He has a large family of now-grown children and is active in community and church affairs. He and his wife, Barbara, divide their time between their ranch in southern Idaho and a winter home (a model low-maintenance house!) in Kauai, Hawaii.